PENGUIN LIFE

ONE DECISION

Mike Bayer, known as Coach Mike to the thousands of clients whose lives he has changed, is a *New York Times* bestselling author, sought-after speaker, and founder and CEO of CAST Centers. Mike is the host of the podcast *Always Evolving with Coach Mike Bayer*, and has appeared on shows such as *The Talk*, *Face the Truth*, *Rachael Ray*, *Dr. Oz*, *The Breakfast Club*, and more. He is a recurring guest expert on *Entertainment Tonight* and a regular contributor to *Psychology Today*. He is also an expert contributor and regular on daytime television's #1 rated show, the *Dr. Phil* show, and is a member of Dr. Phil's advisory board. Mike lives in Los Angeles.

ONE DECISION

The First Step to a Better Life

MIKE BAYER

life

PENGUIN BOOKS
An imprint of Penguin Random House LLC
penguinrandomhouse.com

First published in the United States of America by Viking,
an imprint of Penguin Random House LLC, 2020
Published in Penguin Books 2021

A Penguin Life Book

Illustrations by Mat Hurtado
Photograph by Nicholas Hurtado

ISBN 9780593296035 (paperback)

THE LIBRARY OF CONGRESS HAS CATALOGED THE
HARDCOVER EDITION AS FOLLOWS:
Names: Bayer, Mike, author.
Title: One decision : the first step to a better life / Mike Bayer.
Description: [New York, New York] : Penguin Life, [2020] | Includes
    bibliographical references.
Identifiers: LCCN 2020021245 (print) | LCCN 2020021246 (ebook) |
    ISBN 9780593296011 (hardcover) | ISBN 9780593296028 (ebook)
Subjects: LCSH: Decision making. | Self-actualization (Psychology) |
    Success. | Change (Psychology)
Classification: LCC BF448 .B377 2020 (print) | LCC BF448 (ebook) |
    DDC 153.8/3—dc23
LC record available at https://lccn.loc.gov/2020021245
LC ebook record available at https://lccn.loc.gov/2020021246

Printed in the United States of America
1st Printing

DESIGNED BY MEIGHAN CAVANAUGH

I dedicate this book to those who want better but don't know where to start, to those who feel something is different but haven't yet embraced it, and to those who may have lost themselves a bit but are ready to take the first step to a better life.

CONTENTS

FOREWORD

One Decision. Two very important words and one pivotal concept from Mike Bayer, who has emerged as one of the most important thought leaders of today. A sincere, trusted, authentic friend and colleague, Mike has written *One Decision* to help you consciously shape the rest of your life to be who you are meant to be and, more important, to do it on purpose.

Living in "reactive mode," you may not have known it at the time, but if you take the time to deconstruct the evolution of the major components of your life—career, relationships, where you live, how you live, what you do and feel, how you treat others and allow others to treat you—each and every aspect that defines you can be traced back to One Decision.

Mike lives in "proactive mode" and is on a laser-focused mission to challenge and guide you to recognize, seize, create, and maximize that One Decision in every area, at every upcoming critical moment of your life, to ensure you claim your most powerful, authentic self.

Winners do things losers don't want to do, and Mike has not met a challenge yet that he is not willing to do, especially for someone else. He is a man who focuses on things that matter for people who care.

You are the ultimate beneficiary of Mike's tenacious spirit and passion for helping others, because I know this book you're holding or listening to right now is the key to unlock the rest of your life in ways you could have never imagined.

Simply put, *One Decision* has already started to change your life. I know it changed mine acting as his muse in the honing of *One Decision*. It will change how you live, it will change your trajectory, it will change your velocity. You will feel as though you're sitting across the room from someone who not only "gets you," but also gets how to help you "get you."

Drawing from his deep well of experience as a highly trained life coach, working with thousands of people across all imaginable walks of life, from paupers to princesses, you will have your own "partner in print" to create an action plan that can keep you from having to live one more minute of one more hour of one more day in a life that is less than what you deserve.

Make picking up this new book by my friend Mike Bayer your first new, conscious, intentional One Decision. You will be so glad you did.

Dr. Phil McGraw

ONE DECISION

INTRODUCTION

Who are you?
That's the greatest challenge,
but also the greatest gift.

The decision to be authentic is the most important decision in our lives, but it's not one we make only once; to stay authentic, we have to do it over and over again. We must revisit our connection with our authenticity every day; otherwise we risk losing our grip on life. And sometimes, we must return to a piece of our past in order to sync back up with who we are, especially when that past is informing our current feelings.

Vulnerability is a key ingredient in the recipe for authenticity, and it's never easy. It doesn't come naturally to anyone because of the risk of judgment. What will others think? What will others say? Are you worried about others accepting you for you you are, or do you feel you need to fake it to win approval? Those questions are completely meaningless in the big scheme of life. Ah, but they're tricky. They sneak in the back door and start muttering quietly. We try to ignore them, but what we have to do is confront them. We have to say, "I don't care! I don't care what people think!" But still . . . it's hard. I get it.

In the first chapter of this book, I'm going to ask you to write down the three most authentic decisions you've made in your life. I want to share with you my three as well:

COMING OUT

GETTING SOBER

STARTING MY BUSINESS

I believe that One Decision can change the trajectory of your life.

And in this book, I'm going to guide you through the process of ensuring that your decisions are coming from your true self so that the trajectory is also yours. I want to provide a road map for you so that you don't have to get lost along the way. Getting lost might mean having a career that's inauthentic, or being in an inauthentic relationship, and it might mean looking around and believing everybody else has it figured out so there must be something wrong with you. So you turn to drugs or alcohol, or watching TV nonstop, or food or pornography or whatever. It's all to deal with the pain of living an incongruent, inauthentic life.

What I know for sure is that we must lay down the "shoulds." We must accept ourselves and not worry about whether others do, or what the outcome might look like. And we must be who we are authentically. I hope that in sharing my decisions with you, I can help you see that you don't need to hold yourself to any kind of "should" standard in your own life.

My goal for you as you read this book is to take that step—to live authentically, to be yourself, in every aspect of your life.

I believe if you read this book and make One Decision to live your life as yourself, then it's been a success. Anytime you find yourself up against a new challenge, deciding on a new direction, or desiring a reinvention of your entire life, or just some part of it, you can pick up this book to reconnect with your authenticity, and thus begin to see the opportunities all around you. You can use this book as a tool to snap you out of a mentality that is standing in the way of your progress, or to inspire you to take a risk, to be bold, and to follow your gut. It is meant to be a wake-up call for your spirit, and to give you a blueprint for making decisions about which you can feel good and at peace. And it's also designed to help you discover the freedom to let go, to stop second-guessing yourself, and to rest assured that no matter what you decide, you can have the freedom to let go of the outcome.

I, for one, have read countless self-help books over the years that have deeply inspired and motivated me, but only a few of them have guided me through the work necessary to explore my own inner workings and then take action toward change. I feel I will have done my job as an author if you come away from this book having taken action. We aren't just going to theorize about your life. That's how this book is different. You are going to make actual decisions that will help you create your better life. You will know how to create an action plan that will get you from where you are to where you want to go.

We all have unique definitions of what a "better life" looks like, so we're going to explore what's really important to you, at your core. This book can help you no matter what it is you're trying to achieve or change in your life. For example, if you want to:

- find your purpose

- improve your mental health

- create better relationships

- make more money

- improve your physical health

- enhance your spiritual life

You may finish this book, or you may get only a few chapters in, but just by starting it—whether someone gave it to you, you bought it for yourself, or you borrowed it from the library—you are already making a decision to take the first step. I'm going to work with you as your life coach. And a life coach gives assignments, exercises, or work of some kind to do. I'll guide you through it, and I think you'll love how much you can discover about yourself in the process.

So, let's do this, let's start making authentic decisions so you can begin to live a better life today.

PART 1

FOUNDATION FOR A BETTER LIFE

1

THE DECISION TO BE YOUR BEST SELF

There's something we all do, every one of us, about thirty-five thousand times a day on average. We do it every single second of our waking life. We do it when we're happy, when we're sad, when we're tired, and when we're energized. Sometimes it feels really easy, and sometimes it can feel like pure agony. It's something we do when we're trying to pursue the love of our life, or when we're trying to get away from someone we *thought* was the love of our life. Some people have utilized it to make a lot of money, and some have lost all their money as a result of it. Some people like to do this all by themselves, and some people expect others to do it for them. We often label it as "good" or "bad." It's instinctual, it's intuitive, it can require a lot of action or none at all.

I'm talking about *decisions*.

The majority of those thirty-five thousand daily decisions won't have a critical impact on our lives; I call them autopilot decisions. When I say autopilot, I am talking about the stuff that every human being needs to do. We make a choice to eat, to go to sleep, when to go to the bathroom. Obviously, if you're dealing with issues on this level, then you have to address them first and foremost, because they can threaten your ability to survive. But what we're going to be talking about in this book is how to make conscious decisions that are lined up toward a better life. Because let's face it: a better life doesn't just fall in our laps.

We have to create it!
We have to take action toward it.

As a life coach, I have worked with thousands of clients over the past eighteen years, and their backstories and situations vary widely. I have worked with celebrities, business owners, corporations, homeless individuals, and everyday people. Some have had struggles in their personal lives with relationships, while others were looking to make twice as much money as they were currently making. I have helped people who were making six-figure salaries to become millionaires, and I have helped millionaires simplify their lives and focus on their family rather than on their finances.

But the thing I frequently found was that the changes they needed to make in their life came down to making *authentic decisions*. That is, taking action in their lives, but from the person they truly are at their core.

This book is, in part, about taking that action—about making the kinds of decisions that can put you on a more positive path in life. You are likely making many decisions each and every day that could determine the course of your future. And the common denominator in all of those decisions is you. So I want to bring awareness not just to the kinds of decisions you're making but to *what is driving you* to make those decisions. Why do we make decisions to self-sabotage? Why do we not stay on track with our goals or struggle with thinking patterns for years? If, for example, I make a decision to improve my health but my belief system is that I am incapable of it, I will have to work so much harder. It will not be inspiring, it will not be fun, it will feel like work.

That's what we are going to do together in this book. We are going to identify what is authentic to you, help you get into alignment with that authenticity, and, ultimately, help you make decisions from that place. As a result, I believe that you will feel better and achieve more of what you want in your life and decrease what you do not want.

This book is about the paradigm shift that I believe is vital for us to make right now: I want you to stop thinking about making the best decision for your life and instead to *make the decision as your Best Self*. That is your One Decision. And in the rest of this chapter, I'm going to show you why that's so important. Before we go any further, I want to share with you the four main tenets of this book:

THE ONE DECISION PARADIGM

4 When our decisions are authentic, we can let go and let the universe decide.

3 When we see opportunities, we can make authentic decisions.

2 When we are being our Best Self, we are able to see obstacles as opportunities.

1 The first step to creating a better life for ourselves is to live as our Best Self.

You're going to see the terms "Best Self" and "authentic self" a lot throughout this book. This concept is neither negative nor positive; it's just *you*. It's about being aligned with your truth, and if you believe in a spiritual practice, then it's being aligned with that too. You're unique, you're original, there's no one like you, and there never will be. It's about embracing your essence, your soul, and it's being in the moment—the here and now—with clarity.

This is about how you exist and
how you express yourself.

NOW, IF YOU HAVE READ *BEST SELF: BE YOU, ONLY BETTER*, THEN:

A. You are awesome, and I am so glad that you dug it
enough to buy this book.

B. You are likely aware of the Best Self and Anti-Self
exercises that were in the first two chapters. I
want to recap those exercises briefly, because
they are foundational to the work we're going to
be doing together. Even if you've already done
these exercises, I'd encourage you to refresh your
memory just because they can be so helpful in
connecting with your authentic self.

My goal is to work with you, the reader, the same way I would
as a life coach; in fact, I often use these exact exercises with clients
and in my own life simply because they are so helpful. (You should
know that the exercises in this book are appropriate for any age
and any walk of life.) I also recommend getting a journal so you

have more space to write and a highlighter or a pen so you can mark this sucker up. With *Best Self*, I even had people tagging me online and sharing photos of sections in the book they highlighted. I love seeing that. You can do the same with this book!

I created the Best Self/Anti-Self exercises in *Best Self* to help you understand who you really are—the whole, authentic you that you bring to every area of your life. Just as it's important to identify those parts of you that you feel are most representative of who you are—your Best Self—it's also so important for you to be familiar with the parts of yourself that do not represent you operating at your best. In doing this exercise, you will be able to pinpoint the most authentic parts of yourself, which is an incredibly empowering process. It allows you to discover who you are at a very deep level, at your core. And, as we go forward in this book, it helps you *act* from that core place.

The idea of the Best Self and the Anti-Self was inspired by the metaphor of an angel on one shoulder and a devil on the other. I wanted to explore that concept (and take it out of any religious context) because I think we can all relate to it and we've all seen ourselves behave in one extreme or the other. We often say or think, "I wasn't myself," or "I don't know why I did that," and that's typically when our Anti-Self is in charge. The Anti-Self exercise helps you identify thoughts, feelings, and behaviors that run contrary to your Best Self. It's an easy trap to fall into, to cling to our worst ideas about ourselves and assume that those are our truest selves. But they come from ego or fear, and they are not at all authentic to who we are. These negative perceptions are merely stories: they could have come from your childhood, how you've experienced hurt, pain, and fear, or from situations in life (emotional abuse, neglect, trauma) that created an outlook that takes away from who you truly are.

You do not have to go to the length of actually completing the Best Self/Anti-Self exercises, but I will give you an overview of them so you can understand the basic concepts. The Best Self exercise first has you take a step back and look at yourself from the outside. When we are being our Best Self, we feel aligned with life, and we feel we are "operating at our best." For me, I consider my Best Self to be very wise, grounded, creative, spiritual, optimistic, compassionate, fun, and clever. My Best Self is not thrown by anything; he's calm and secure. In *Best Self,* after we clearly defined the most authentic parts of ourselves, we created a drawing or image that represents our Best Self. Mine is a wizard named Merlin. I chose a wizard because, in my mind, wizards are creatively and powerfully brilliant. Merlin is representative of how I feel when I am aligned with who I really am. Merlin comes in incredibly handy when I need to live in faith, and when I am handling adversity. Connecting with Merlin helps me to be completely honest. I wish I could operate as Merlin all the time! But as we know, life is constantly moving and changing. In that, new stressors and challenges can throw us off, and our Anti-Self might even get triggered.

Even when life is going great, we still struggle from time to time with our ego, fear, anxiety, stress, depression, and anger. And while those are real struggles, they are not an authentic part of who we are. Those things happen to us, but they *are not us*. I'll also share with you that one of my Anti-Selves (because we all have more than one) is named Angelos, and he often arises from some form of fear. Sometimes it's a fear of failing, not being prepared, or having to face uncomfortable feelings. When Angelos is calling the shots, I find myself pushing people away. I do this because that part of me wants to be left alone, and in that state I find myself to be insufferable. I get stuck in the problem, I'm easily annoyed, and I become unenjoyable company, even to myself!

As you'll notice in this illustration, Angelos is a male witch. I chose a male witch because, like a wizard, this fictional character is typically capable of magic, but in Angelos's case he cannot cast any spells.

The process of creating our Anti-Self is powerful because it lets us add elements of humor to the parts of ourselves that we really don't like, and in so doing, we create new energy around them. How often do we look at parts of ourselves that we loathe but feel powerless to change them? We just assume that's "how we're wired," or we're "just like our parents," or we chalk it up to some other element over which we have no control. But when we create and flesh out our Anti-Self, we suddenly have a tool for bringing those elements of ourselves to life so that we can, in fact, control them. We are no longer slaves to our lesser qualities, falling prey to self-sabotaging behavior. Instead, we make a caricature out of those elements, giving us a new level of awareness and even power over them, an ability to view them with renewed objectivity, and thus an ability to quell those tendencies and choose to let our Best Self take over.

Here's the key, and the reason Best Self/Anti-Self is so fundamental to how we take action to improve our lives: our Best Self is able to perceive opportunities where our Anti-Self sees only obstacles. Those are universal qualities to all Best Selves and Anti-Selves. When we are being our Best Self, we believe that no matter how bad our external circumstances are, there are still opportunities available to us. When we are being our Anti-Self, or in other words when we are being inauthentic, we focus on the problems and fail to see the possibilities for growth. This is also when we fight, flee, freeze, or appease, but when we are not actually in danger.

YOU'VE MADE AUTHENTIC DECISIONS BEFORE

I think it's a good starting place to realize you've already made plenty of decisions as your Best Self. In the introduction, I shared with you some decisions I've made as my Best Self, so now let's take some time to look at past decisions that you believe were in your best interest, and that resulted in a positive outcome, so that you can begin to attribute this good decision-making quality to yourself.

Looking back across the span of your life up to this moment in time, think about three decisions you made that you'd categorize as decisions you made from your Best Self, decisions that you felt were aligned with who you are, even if only in retrospect. Maybe you decided to go to college and it opened up career opportunities to you. Perhaps you got married and you feel that was in your best interest. I'll pause here to say that even if a marriage ended, but you took something positive from it, you can still think of that as a good decision. Maybe you decided not to do something, and you're very happy you made that choice because it could've been harmful to you. When you really get into it, you might discover there are thousands of decisions you've made that have led you toward a better life, and if you'd like to write more than three, by all means please do!

When you become aware of, and take credit for, these authentic decisions you have made in the past, you tell your brain that you are able to make decisions as your Best Self. For some, perhaps it's about choosing integrity over money. For others, it could be choosing to go to therapy instead of ignoring festering emotional issues. Maybe you've decided not to sell yourself short in some situation. It could be that you made the decision to get sober or help someone else get sober. Maybe it was marrying someone, or maybe it was divorcing someone. The point is, let's charge up your decision-making battery by recognizing that you are capable of making life choices that have been in your own best interest.

MY *BETTER LIFE* DECISIONS THUS FAR:

_____

_____

_____

_____

_____

_____

_____

_____

_____

_____

If you're being honest with yourself about your better life decisions above, it is likely you can look at this list and feel proud. A list like this helps us feel better because we can see the truth of what we have chosen that has led to a better life. Consider all the positive ripples of change that came from each of these decisions; it's tremendous! That's because when you made them, you were aligned with your values, and you generated positive change in your life.

YOU'RE ONE DECISION AWAY

If you're currently living in darkness, or feeling completely overwhelmed, I get it—both on a personal level and on a professional one. Maybe you're in a time of your life where it feels as if your world has come crashing down, or the walls are closing in, and you don't know what to do next. Perhaps a long-term relationship recently came to an unexpected end. Or maybe a loved one passed away and they were your rock. It could be the loss of a job, and you had no backup plan. Or it might be a diagnosis or a drastic decline in your physical health. Or you may just be really depressed. If something like this has happened in your life, and you're feeling consumed by the intensity of it all,

I want you to know that you are One Decision away from allowing the universe to deliver joy back into your life.

Your first step, which is universal to all of us and to every situation, is to find the opportunity. Because as long as we're living and breathing, I believe there is always an opportunity within every obstacle we face. Regardless of where you're starting from, the journey you're embarking upon is one of hope, of joy, and of reconnecting with your Best Self. You deserve to have peace and to experience happiness in your life again, and you will get there. You may not be able to see the opportunities yet, and that's okay. The fact that you decided to start reading this book, and that you are open to the ideas within it, is a great start.

GETTING INTO ALIGNMENT

I've spent more than eighteen years of my career helping people make authentic decisions, and in so doing, via obsessive research, coaching sessions, and introspection, I've discovered one fundamental and universal truth. If we are connected with our spirituality when making any given decision, we are infinitely more likely to make a decision that will lead us toward a better life rather than away from it. When I talk about the universe deciding outcomes in our life, the "universe" in that context refers to the forces outside our own personal control, whatever you believe that might be.

Decisions we make that are rooted in our authentic beliefs and values are the decisions we can look back on years later and see as ones that shaped us. They took us on a trajectory that feels right, the life path on which we were meant to walk. If you are

Christian—whether Catholic or Protestant, or another variation of that faith—then your belief system might align with what Jesus would do, or what the Bible would say. If you are Muslim, then your beliefs will most likely be based on the teachings of the Koran. If you are Jewish, then yours may be derived from the Torah. If you're part of a 12-step program, then your belief system may include some of the above or you may believe in a higher power whom you do not name. Perhaps you believe in energy such as karma, or you subscribe to some other spiritual belief system that is in alignment with how you choose to exist in this world as your Best Self. Even if you're an atheist or you say that you have nothing spiritual to hold on to, I would invite you to think of your spirituality as your moral compass, as your decisions about what is right and what is wrong, at what is aligned with your value system, and your belief about what is possible when you're being your authentic self.

Regardless, if you tap into your authentic spiritual beliefs and practices when you make decisions, you will have more clarity.

Decisions will be easier to make.

Let's make a commitment while working through *One Decision* to bring in our spiritual practice. As I touched on earlier in this chapter, my Best Self is a wizard. To me, this belief in myself is a spiritual one. I have such a clear vision of that "wizard" within me that when I need to make a decision, I can easily call upon him and make an authentic one. I want you to be able to do the same. I write books with that very objective: that you will be able to vividly identify aspects of yourself.

GET FASCINATED WITH YOURSELF

You likely don't put yourself in the list of the top one hundred most fascinating people in the world. I get it. No one really thinks of themselves as all that fascinating or intriguing. But you are! We live with ourselves day in and day out, so it's a little like old hat. So, cringe all you want: I'm telling you that it's time to get fascinated with YOU. There are so many layers to you, and so many interesting reasons why you do the things you do. And you will need to learn about those layers to do the work ahead in this book.

If you're worried this is going to turn you into a self-centered, bigheaded monster, no need. There's a big difference between what's called narcissistic personality disorder (NPD) and just being really fascinated with yourself. In the same way, there's a big difference between having anxiety and being diagnosed with an anxiety disorder. Most likely if you're reading this, you don't have NPD, because if you did, you'd think you had all the answers and wouldn't need to read a self-help book!

When I became an alcohol and drug abuse counselor, I probably read a hundred books in order to learn everything I needed in order to counsel those in recovery. Then I did 880 internship hours because that's when you take what you've learned and practice it in the real world. It's just like when you're getting a driver's permit: first, you learn in a classroom setting and read at home, and then you go out and practice on the road. Right now, I'm taking Portuguese (a tough language to learn!). I take a lesson, and then I have to practice or else I start to lose the knowledge I gained. *Eu devo praticar!* (That means "I must practice!") What I'm saying is that I want you to be a sponge, to learn about yourself and the world around you, and then put your knowledge into practice to better your life. The "knowing" is not enough. It's the knowing *and* the doing that will get you where you want to go.

Because I'll be helping you to make decisions in your life that are grounded in your spirituality, I want you to write down one thing that you can do while working on this book that will align you spiritually. What is something you can practice that is going to make you feel spiritually aligned? This isn't about what your family or someone else might recommend, but what resonates with *you*.

This part might be really easy for you, or you might struggle. If you know the answer right off the bat, great! If not, I'm including a list of some practices from which you can choose. Write your answer below.

LIST OF COMMON SPIRITUAL PRACTICES

- meditating

- praying
- saying or creating a mantra
- practicing deep breathing
- walking or hiking in nature
- dancing

- singing
- exercising
- creating a gratitude list
- doing a guided visualization exercise

A practice that makes me feel aligned with my spirituality is:

_____

The practice you wrote down will likely evolve as we work through this book together. My own practice has changed over time, for sure. The point is to try a few different things until you discover what it is that quiets your mind and allows your spirit to take the lead.

NIKKO'S ONE DECISION MOMENT

I believe in my Best Self so much I actually had it tattooed on my arm as a constant reminder. In case you don't know, tattoos are intimate experiences because you spend a lot of time with your tattoo artist. The artist who did my tattoo is Nikko Hurtado, and I really enjoyed getting to know him through the process of having Merlin tattooed on my arm. He's very passionate about his art form, and given that millions of people follow him on social media, and his artwork is being dis-  played in the Museum of Pop Culture, his unique gift resonates with others. Nikko shared with me one of his top authentic decisions he's made in his life, and I am excited to now share it with you. Here's his story.

When Nikko was twelve, he went to live with his grandmother Lucy, and he credits her with raising him. He remembers his grandma as "an angel" who took in people who needed care without question, including two of her grandkids whom she raised. Lucy's door was always open to friends and family in need.

Nikko and his grandma shared a special bond. They understood each other, and she was always encouraging him. He says she was the best friend he ever had. Nikko struggled in school but had a passion for art that began at a young age, and Lucy fostered that passion. He often took classes at the Pasadena ArtCenter with a good friend. But Nikko had a rebellious streak, and rather than completing high school, he took a job in construction and gave up art. Lucy, always supportive and never one to push, gave Nikko the space he needed to find his own way.

The friend who had gone to art classes with Nikko soon opened up a tattoo shop. Nikko went to visit him, and the friend asked if he'd ever thought about tattooing. Nikko had not considered it but was intrigued. His friend offered him an apprenticeship on the spot. Nikko quit his job in construction and started at the tattoo shop the very next day. He says, "My life changed from that very moment. I felt like tattooing kind of chose me. I knew I was meant to do it."

At that time, Nikko and his family lived in lower-middle-class neighborhoods and had modest means. That is, until his grandmother won $6.2 million in the California lottery. As you might imagine, this drastically changed the family dynamic, and not for the better. Everyone wanted in on the winnings. Over time, a rift formed in the family, and when Lucy passed away a few years later, there was a vicious legal battle over the remaining money. Nikko's mom was the head of the trust, but the rest of the family contested it, had it overturned, and left her homeless. They literally kicked her out on the street.

By then, Nikko had opened his own tattoo shop, and business was going decently well. Though he'd had a strained relationship with his mother for most of his life, he rented an apartment for her and brought his siblings into his business. Of his mom, he said, "I've tried to work on the relationship because you only get one mom. Ultimately, I know everyone is just doing their best, including her."

He wanted nothing to do with the lottery winnings or the members of his family who were greedily fighting over them, so he made his One Decision to walk away from all of it. Being true to his Best Self, Nikko says he chose integrity over money. He believes that decision (as well as his "guardian angel" Lucy) is the reason his business and life have been so blessed. He had no plan B, nothing to fall back on, but he knew in his heart that he was going to make it work. He said, "I never wanted to be in a situation where I had to depend on someone else's money like my family was."

I asked what happened to the family members who had fought so hard over the winnings, and he shook his head and said, "It's really sad. They're all dying off now. And the irony is that in the end the lawyers got all the money anyway. Every penny."

Today, Nikko operates his business and every aspect of his life from his Best Self. And he has learned some valuable lessons on his journey to this point. He's a pioneer in the area of realism in tattoo artistry, and for anyone who makes an impact like that, a lot of attention comes with it. When he first started really getting noticed in the industry for the images he was creating, a fellow artist, Guy Aitchison, pulled him aside and pointed something out. Here's how Nikko recalls it: "I used to drink and party like an animal. I was super arrogant, and was just living and not really thinking anyone was paying attention. But when I was twenty-five, Guy told me I had to watch what I do because I was leading by example. I didn't understand what he meant, until I saw someone else in our community acting the same way I was, and that person told me that he just wanted to 'be like me.' That really hit home, and I saw the negative effect I could have. I didn't want that at all, so I consciously decided not to drink or smoke from that point on, and I really aim to be a positive influence for others."

Nikko now says that tattooing is not his primary art form. He believes his true art is inspiring others. That is his calling. He remembers telling his high school sweetheart, who is now his wife, when they were just fifteen years old that he was going to be something great. She'd say, "What, though? What are you going to be?" He'd reply, "I don't know, I can just feel it in my gut." But then he'd go to school and other kids would tease him and call him a loser. "Someone said to me, 'What are you going to be, some kind of tattoo artist?' Like, it was meant to be so demeaning. Well, guess what? Now I own two shops, my business is successful, and it's because I didn't let those words, those labels, determine the direction of my life. Instead, I let them inspire me. I say, let people be your biggest cheerleaders, even if they are trying to tear you down. The biggest reward is deciding not to be angry at those people, but instead to take the step forward, take action. Now I can look back and basically say thank you to those people. It doesn't matter what label you are given. It's what you *choose* to be that matters."

When his little brother was just sixteen years old and working at Target, Nikko wanted him to have a skill he could use so that he too could create a better life for himself. He offered to teach him how to draw. I asked him if you can really teach someone to be an artist, and he said, "The simplest way I can put it is this: anyone can learn how to play basketball. But there are some talents that are innate. We can learn the technical aspects of it, the 'rules,' and then we can play pretty well, but not everyone can be Michael Jordan. Art is a visual language. Just like you can learn to speak French, you can learn to draw. You just have to learn how to read, understand what you're looking at, and start with square one." So that's what he did for his brother, who is now a fantastic tattoo artist in his own right.

There's no doubt Nikko has made decisions about how he perceives life and about who he is in the world that have kept him on the path he believes he was meant to walk. But I was curious if regret played any role in his decision making. When I asked him about it, he said, "I had a friend once who asked me to get a matching tattoo with him, and for whatever reason I said no. But he ended up passing away. You don't regret the things you do; you regret the things you don't do. So, even though he was gone, some friends and I went and got that tattoo—matching black anchors. It was a sort of a traditional tattooing symbol—makes you think of sailors going from port to port. I used to feel like that myself, like a sailor traveling the world and doing my thing, living the way I wanted, going wherever the sea was taking me. That tattoo has kept me grounded; it's a constant reminder of family and friends.

When we got it, we promised that we would bring each other back to reality if we ever got lost."

As a young man, Nikko had often told his grandmother he wanted to have a daughter and name her Lucy in her honor, even though she told him not to; she was far too humble to embrace such an idea. But he did it anyway, and now his beautiful daughter is a daily reminder of the selflessness and unconditional love consistently displayed by his grandmother.

Nikko believes everyone has something inside of them they know they're supposed to do. He says, "That's the point of life. By my not doing what everyone said, I have a better life because I didn't follow the system. I didn't behave the way most of my family chose to. I didn't listen to the labels assigned to me. I made my own decision. And never looked back."

Nikko's story is so inspiring to me. It exemplifies a lot of what we're going to talk about in this book, primarily allowing our Best Self to guide our decision making. The truth is, you've let your Best Self be your decision-making guide before. Many times. As you discovered earlier in this chapter, you have made decisions from the authentic, spirit-led place within you before. Maybe it was by accident, or maybe you set an intention around it. You've seen yourself do it before, and you'll see yourself do it again, but this time with even more knowledge and intention.

What I intend to do is to help you create your own specific method for making decisions that contribute positively to your life. Let's tap into the unique aspects of yourself to put your decision-making power firmly in your hands.

2

THE FOUR *O*s

Have you ever felt totally stuck, unable to make a change because you felt overwhelmed by the possibilities? Have you ever wondered why certain things get in your way of creating more peace, love, or success in your life? Why it seems as if you can so easily get thrown by a problem, and make decisions that aren't in your best interest? Have you ever made a decision that you just knew, at a gut level, was not in keeping with who you really are? In this chapter, we're going to take a look at how you could be letting problems, or in this case obstacles, get in the way of living the life you truly want.

As we've discussed, your first step is to define your Best Self. Once you have stepped into that awareness of your authentic Best Self, your next step is to view your life through that optic, or lens, of who you really are. We have to solve problems every day; that's just the nature of life. And we have to compromise every day. You can still be authentic and compromise.

You can still be authentic and disagree with someone.

I believe that one major issue that keeps us stuck in indecision, or in a pattern of decisions that are not in our best interest, is that we tend to be too focused on a desired outcome. We let the outcome be in the driver's seat. Here, I want to bring us back to our One Decision Paradigm:

THE ONE DECISION PARADIGM

1. The first step to creating a better life for ourselves is to live as our Best Self.

2. When we are being our Best Self, we are able to see obstacles as opportunities.

3. When we see opportunities, we can make authentic decisions.

4. When our decisions are authentic, we can let go and let the universe decide.

In this paradigm the outcome has to come last. The outcome of your decisions does not define you; because we can't truly control it, it simply doesn't make sense that it should play any role whatsoever in your authentic decision making. When there's a problem we can turn into an opportunity, we feel better, which allows us to make decisions that are better for our lives. And therefore, whatever the outcome is, we still feel good.

I define success as being ourselves. That's it! Why would we have been created as ourselves if we were meant to be someone else? We weren't created to people please. We are who we are, and we are going to be the happiest and most fulfilled in our lives when we are living as that person.

I believe that all the decisions we make throughout each day of our lives can lead us toward a better life or *away* from it. Regardless of how "big" or "small" any decision might seem to be on the surface, all decisions have the potential to improve our life if we are making them as our Best Self. This is the crux of why it's in our best interest to learn how we are viewing our life, so we can begin to make authentic decisions.

We never know what seemingly insignificant decision might lead us down an entirely new path, toward something more amazing than we could have ever imagined. Likewise, we often put so much pressure on ourselves to make what we think are enormous, even life-changing decisions that turn out not to have the impact we expected. Since we can't predict the outcome of any given decision, we must ensure that we are approaching them from within our Best Self. And right now, I'm going to show you how you can do just that through the power of something I refer to as the Four Os:

OBSTACLE

OPPORTUNITY

ONE DECISION

OUTCOME

OBSTACLE

OBSTACLE: A thing that we perceive as blocking our way, preventing or hindering our progress.

How we perceive a person, place, or thing will determine what choices we make. When we see a problem as something not solvable, we're seeing it as an obstacle.

Think of a pair of sunglasses. The lenses filter light in specific ways so that our eyes are protected when we're in bright sunlight. Some lenses change the color of the light; for example, blue lenses make everything we look at appear to be some shade of blue. Imagine putting on a pair of sunglasses, and one of the lenses is the "obstacle" lens. When we view something through that obstacle lens, in the same way the blue lens made everything blue, the obstacle lens makes everything in life appear to be an obstacle. Through that lens, we can't see it as anything other than something we must solve, overcome, or allow to stop us altogether.

Any perceived problem is going to continue to be a problem if we look at it as an obstacle. Furthermore, being in the obstacle doesn't *feel* good to us. It makes us feel bad in myriad ways.

● **When we're viewing something as an obstacle, we tend to**

- blame

- make excuses

- complain

- feel sorry for ourselves (victim mentality)

- stay stuck

- not forgive ourselves or others

- obsess

- feel fearful

- feel insecure

- feel stressed or anxious
- feel depressed
- feel lonely
- feel resentful
- justify

VICTIM TO VICTOR

If there are any areas of your life where you're currently blaming people, places, or things for something that isn't going right for you, this is the time to move from playing victim to being the victor. It could be that you've been a victim of some very unfortunate events. When those things occur, if we allow ourselves to remain a victim, we are giving away power to the person, place, or thing that isn't serving us. When we are a victor, we get our power back. It's a power within ourselves that is a choice, a decision.

The reason why it's so imperative to get this mindset under control now is that we want to be clear that we are not making any decisions out of spite or passive-aggressiveness. We've all been in a victim mindset to some degree at some point in our lives, and very often it's because we are looking for just cause for why something isn't going well in our life. We want to look outside ourselves, to point the finger at someone else for not protecting us, for not helping us, or for deceiving or hurting us. But you're in this incredible moment right now, where you are about to exercise your power to change your life for the better, and I don't want you to let a victim mentality steal this opportunity away from you.

So, as you think about the decisions you're making today, ask yourself if there's any part of you that's doing them because you're angry at someone or something else for your current circumstances. To get a better idea whether you might be approaching any current decisions from within a victim mindset, take a look at the chart below. Does your thinking fall in the "Victim Mentality" column or the "Victor Mentality" column?

VICTIM MENTALITY	VICTOR MENTALITY
Blaming others for your emotions.	Owning your ability to control your own emotions.
Cynical or pessimistic thinking.	Opportunity-minded/ optimistic.
Finding things to complain about, even when things go right.	Finding the silver lining, and expressing gratitude even when things go wrong.
Thinking life is against you.	Knowing the universe has your back.

(continued)

VICTIM MENTALITY	VICTOR MENTALITY
Feeling powerless, or unable to cope.	Finding the tools you need to cope with anything that occurs.
Putting yourself down.	Believing in yourself, acting as your Best Self.
Needing sympathy from others.	Being kind and compassionate toward yourself and others.
Saying or thinking "you," like "you made me feel bad," or "you did this to me."	Replacing "you" with "I," and owning your part in anything that happens, good or bad.
Feeling sorry for yourself, and seeming to enjoy it.	Feeling proud of your abilities, and acknowledging your positive traits.

Left unchecked, a victim mentality can easily form into deep resentments, which are detrimental to our overall well-being. If you have found yourself existing in a state of resentment over something that has happened to you, I know that can be a tough wall to climb, but it is absolutely possible.

OPPORTUNITY

OPPORTUNITY: A set of circumstances that makes it *possible* to do something.

Opportunity is the lens that allows us to see possibility. When we look at life through the opportunity lens, we are suddenly able to see chances for growth, learning, discovering something new, going in a new direction, trying out new skills, and so on. Those opportunities were completely invisible to us through the obstacle lens. You might be thinking, "Isn't this just a version of looking at life through rose-colored glasses?" The difference is that rose-colored glasses change our perception only temporarily, where-as opportunity lenses lead us to make a decision and follow it up with action. The truth is, within every obstacle that comes our way, there is a multitude of opportunities that we can seize upon;

we simply have to be willing to look at them through the opportunity lens.

It feels better to us when we are in the opportunity mindset. It feels authentic to us, because remember, our Best Self, our most authentic self, is made up of only positive attributes. So when we're bogged down in the obstacle, we are not being our Best Self. But switching into opportunity mindset is a quick way to reconnect with our authenticity.

- **When we view something as an opportunity, we tend to**
  - be optimistic
  - think in a solution-oriented way
  - feel better emotionally and mentally
  - accept responsibility
  - think outside the box
  - learn something new
  - grow as a human

OBSTACLE V. OPPORTUNITY EXAMPLE

Let's walk through an example scenario and look at it first as an obstacle and then as an opportunity, and discuss the One Decision you could make within each. Let's say you've hit financial hard times, and you retired a couple years ago.

With the obstacle outlook, you might think
- I'm not qualified to reenter the workforce.
- I'll never make ends meet with the kind of job I could land.
- I didn't love working even when I was doing it full-time; I definitely won't love it this time around.
- I only know how to do one thing, and there are no jobs in the field right now.
- I'm so mad at myself I let this happen, and devastated to have to give up my retirement.

Whereas, using an opportunity outlook, you might think
- If I do a little research, I might find out about job options for my age range.
- Who knows—maybe I'll even enjoy myself more than I did in my last career!
- I'm going to just go with the flow and look for a job, and maybe I'll make some new friends along the way.
- It's actually a little exciting to think about learning something new.

(continued)

When we look at situations like needing to go back to work as an obstacle, you can see how it doesn't lead us anywhere worthwhile. It leaves us feeling bad, and sorry for ourselves. It creates negative energy that can impact the rest of our day, and maybe several areas of our life. And worst of all, that negative outlook can stop us from taking action.

However, you can see how looking at it through an opportunity lens creates new, fresh energy. It opens our eyes to possibilities, to new directions. It helps us move forward as our Best Self, instead of being stuck in negativity. The more we can see opportunities instead of obstacles, the more we can enjoy and improve our lives.

ONE DECISION

ONE DECISION: A conclusion or resolution reached from within one's Best Self.

Once we've chosen to view something as an opportunity, explored the possibilities, and aligned with our Best Self, it's time to make our One Decision. Following through on our One Decision will require us to make many "uniting decisions," which will strengthen and support our One Decision and make it a reality.

ONE DECISION AS OBSTACLE V. OPPORTUNITY

Let's continue the example of needing to go back to work, and see what type of One Decision you might reach based on whether you approach it as an obstacle or as an opportunity.

With the obstacle outlook, you might decide to

- Go into denial and indecision, and let the financial situation worsen to the point of needing to declare bankruptcy before taking any action.
- Limit yourself to looking for only one type of job that doesn't fire you up.
- Have a bad attitude at any job interviews, and get rejected as a result.
- Turn to self-sabotaging or numbing behavior to block out your reality.
- Become depressed, and begin to isolate yourself from others.

With the opportunity outlook, you might decide to

- Ask your family to help you research ideas for jobs that might be right for you.
- Try talking to people at all the places you regularly visit, and let them know you're looking for a job so that you can begin networking.
- Practice your interview skills for an hour every day.

(continued)

- Update your résumé.
- Apply for jobs online.
- Start learning a new skill that interests you.
- Spend some time in your spiritual practice of choice, to reconnect more deeply with your spirituality as you move forward in this new direction in your life.

As you can see, the One Decision that you will arrive at differs greatly depending on how you approach it—whether as an obstacle or opportunity. Isn't it incredible what can happen with a simple shift in perception?

OUTCOME

OUTCOME: The way something turns out, a consequence over which we have no actual control.

We can control the One Decision we make, but once we make it, we must let go because from that point onward, the ***universe decides*** the outcome.

We cannot predict outcomes, no matter how hard we try. Even when we think we've made the exact right decision and it came from our Best Self, the outcome can still turn out to be something completely unexpected. The goal is to feel good about the decision, regardless of the outcome. When we change, our decisions change. Importantly, when we operate as our Best Self, we don't second-guess and think later that we *should have* handled it differently.

In fact, I think of the word "should" as a curse word. "Should" is very dangerous. Why? Well, think about anytime you've used that word in a sentence, whether it's one you said out loud or just in your head. Very rarely is it used to enhance our lives. When we focus on something we "should" have done, we are looking at the past through a prism of regret. We're implying that we did something wrong. I've met so many people who have gotten stuck in the past, and every time life throws them a curveball, they immediately look back and say, "I should've done this or that." And often we direct it at someone else—"you should have done this," or "you should do this instead of what you're doing." Does that ever end well? Nope. It makes them miserable, and us too. So, as we move through this process, just keep in mind that there's absolutely no room for "should" on this journey.

Instead of getting stuck in that "should" spiral, we can have peace with the choice we made because we relied on the guidance of our authenticity, and we chose to see all the opportunities in front of us in making the decision. We will be more prepared for the ultimate outcome. Regardless of what the universe decides that outcome will be, we always feel better about it if we choose to view life as an opportunity.

Within these Os, there can be so much freedom for you:

- freedom from fear of making the wrong decision

- freedom from cycles of indecision

- freedom from regret that you made the wrong decision

Understanding these concepts and the driving forces behind them can give you the ability to make confident choices that are in your best interest.

TRY ON A NEW PAIR OF SHADES

Right now, let's take these concepts out for a spin with a specific example. You can think about it as trying on different pairs of sunglasses. The first colors everything in your field of vision as an obstacle.

Let's say you want to lose weight. If you're looking at it as an obstacle, then how might you feel?

OBSTACLE: I WANT TO LOSE WEIGHT, BUT I . . .

- don't have time to research the right diet
- don't have the money to pay for a trainer or nutritionist

- haven't been able to lose weight in the past, so that must mean I'm not capable

How does that feel? Not great, right? You paint yourself into a corner with the obstacle optic. There's nowhere to go from those statements or beliefs.

Now, through that obstacle optic, what kind of decision might you make as a result?

OBSTACLE: I WANT TO LOSE WEIGHT, BUT I'M GOING TO . . .

- do nothing about it because it's too hard

- gripe about how much weight I need to lose

- wish my circumstances were different

- beat myself up about it

You might notice that none of those decisions can lead you to losing any weight. Looking at it through the optic of an obstacle is extremely limiting.

Now let's try to look at your desire to lose weight as an opportunity instead. Put on your opportunity sunglasses and consider the difference.

OPPORTUNITY: I WANT TO LOSE WEIGHT. I . . .

- can talk to friends who have successfully lost weight to see how they did it

- can look into free activities I might actually enjoy

- can research small changes to make in my everyday habits

- keep a positive outlook

This optic opens up many more possibilities. The obstacle optic is like tunnel vision. It doesn't allow for us to see anything other than obstacles. But when we simply choose to look at it through the opportunity optic, a new world of possibility opens up.

What kind of decision might you make when viewing your desire to lose weight through the opportunity optic?

OPPORTUNITY: I WANT TO LOSE WEIGHT, SO I WILL . . .

- eat only between the hours of 8:00 a.m. and 7:00 p.m.

- eat more vegetables and fruits, and cut out sugary drinks

- go on daily walks

- check in with friends who have gone through a similar journey

Now it's your turn. First, write down something you're looking to change in your life. Maybe it's a problem, or something you want more of in your life. Whatever it is you want to accomplish, write it here:

_____

_____

_____

_____

Next, write down how you've been feeling about it when you look at it through the optic of **obstacle**.

_____

_____

_____

_____

_____

Now, what's a **decision** you've made or could make if you're choosing to look at it through the optic of obstacle?

_____

_____

_____

_____

_____

Okay, next, let's look at it through the optic of **opportunity**. How do you feel about it when you look at it in this way?

_____

_____

_____

_____

_____

Now, what's a **decision** you can make when you choose to look at it through the optic of opportunity?

_____

_____

_____

_____

_____

It's important to note that this might have come easily to you, or you might feel stumped. If you're stumped, don't worry. In part 2 of this book, we're going to dig deeper and delve into the FORCEs that could be keeping you strictly in that obstacle optic and preventing you from seeing the opportunities. These can easily become patterns, and we will work together to uproot those patterns and get you into opportunity mode.

HELP FROM OTHERS

When it comes to making authentic decisions, we all need a little help from others. Later in the book, we're going to talk about how to create your One Decision team, which is meant to help you make decisions as your Best Self. A solid team will help you take action and it will support you, no matter the outcome. I'll show you how to assemble your team so that you know exactly who to turn to when you need a hand.

USING THE FORCE TO SWITCH FROM OBSTACLE TO OPPORTUNITY

It's very likely that you have identified obstacles standing in your way of that change before, even if only on a subconscious level.

Maybe you've been telling yourself for a long time that you wish you could change something about your life but you "can't because _____." Whatever comes after "because" is your obstacle, or obstacles.

"I wish I could have a fulfilling relationship, but I can't because _____."

"I'd like to spend more time with my loved ones, but I can't because _____."

"I wish I could make more money, but I can't because _____."

"I'd give anything to feel less lonely all the time, but I can't because _____."

"If only I could be physically healthy, but I can't because _____."

I could ask you to write down everything that comes after your own "because" right now, but I want to hold off on that. The prevailing logic is to identify what problems are in your way so that you can get busy solving them, and then—voilà!—life changes. There's only one problem with that approach. If we don't get to the root cause, or the reason why we viewed that thing as an obstacle in the first place, we won't be able to make lasting change in our lives because we end up repeating a pattern and we aren't sure why we keep ending up with the same issues. We'll solve that particular obstacle, sure, but what happens next time? And the next? The problem/solution dynamic hasn't worked in the past, or else you would still be using it to better your life right now. We need something more. We need to go deeper and discover how we can switch permanently out of the obstacle state of mind and get into an *opportunity* state of mind. Once you have the tools for doing that, a whole new world will open up to you.

So, the first step is for us to shift our perspective on obstacles and choose to see the opportunities within them. But how do we make that switch from "obstacle" to "opportunity"? It starts by understanding that there is a powerful, invisible FORCE at play. This FORCE can obscure our vision and keep us from being able to see opportunities if we allow it to do so. Let me explain.

If you've ever seen the film series *Star Wars*, then you are familiar with a concept called the Force. The Force is a spiritual energy field that binds the galaxy together, and certain living beings have the ability to tap into it and use it for good or for evil. The more trained they are at accessing that energy, the more powerful they become. Using the Force, they can play tricks on people's minds (that is, "Jedi mind tricks"), levitate objects, and see premonitions of the future. When it comes to real life, there is also an invisible force that has a powerful effect on our decision-making behavior, but what's incredibly exciting is, just like the Jedis, we have the ability to use that force in wonderful ways.

We are going to take a deep dive into the FORCE a little later in this book, but for now I want you to know that many of us have been hoodwinked, in a way, believing that we are seeing the whole picture of our lives, but in reality our vision has been obscured by the negative side of the FORCE. This is often the reason we haven't made positive changes up to this point: we cannot see the opportunities before us; we can see *only* the obstacles.

We've all felt the effects of the FORCE in other people. For example, think about someone whom you would categorize as a "pessimist," or a "negative person." When someone like that walks into a room, we can literally feel that energy around them. They might always be "one-upping" others with their misery—like, "Oh, you think that's bad? Listen to what horrible thing happened to me!" It's that classic glass-half-empty mentality where they just can't seem to find much good in their life at all. If you've ever seen that in action, you know how much that energy can affect other people; it can drag you down in a hurry. You might even feel more anxious or depressed around someone like this, because that energy is contagious.

On the other hand, perhaps you've come across an optimist who also has critical thinking—in other words, someone with an optimistic viewpoint, but not to the point of being delusional! Think of someone who is just bubbling over with positive energy. No matter what life dishes up to this kind of person, they have an uncanny ability to always find the silver lining and make lemonade out of lemons. That's also a *very* powerful energy. You might find yourself always feeling better after having encountered someone like this, uplifted and light on your feet. Perhaps the conversations you have with him or her always seem upbeat, and you are inspired and motivated by them.

Both of those are examples of the FORCE. It is truly an energy, and it affects us as well as others. You might have always assumed that certain people are just "hardwired" to be negative or positive, but I know we have a choice. People *do* change. We can choose to rewire ourselves and tap into positive energy forces. That rewiring process is all about shifting from obstacles into opportunities. When certain mindsets are deeply ingrained, our first step is to identify and understand the mindset for what it is, and *then* choose a new one. That's the work we will do in the second part of this book as we delve deeper into the FORCE.

For now, I want you to bring awareness to the fact that we, all of us, have the *ability* to shift from obstacle to opportunity, and make our One Decision accordingly. I know this is a huge game changer.

3

ENVISIONING YOUR "BETTER LIFE"

If I were to ask you, "What do you truly want in your life?" or "What do you want more of in your life?" would you have an answer? Our impulse answers are so often the stories we've been telling ourselves, and some of those stories may be true, but what I've found is the majority of people I've worked with have no idea what they *really* want. They usually do not know what they truly want because they are looking outside themselves instead of focusing on what is inside. For example, I have worked with people who say they want to make more money, but what they truly desire is more security in their life. Some people say they want a better job, but what they're really looking for is a purpose. In this chapter, I'll help you get underneath those external desires and into the truth of what you authentically want in your life.

Not to be a buzzkill, but this begins with having a realistic vision of our lives. In life, we have a choice. We can go toward where the momentum is, or we can keep trying to force it. If you've ever watched one of those music or dance competition shows on television, you know that there are some with that "star" quality, that "it" factor, and there are others who just do not have what it takes to make a career out of performing. And that doesn't make them any less valuable as human beings; it just means they need to be realistic about what direction they are going in life. And that's our job now—to understand what a realistic vision for our "better life" looks like. Once we have that vision, we can set ourselves up for success.

WHAT DO YOU *REALLY* WANT?

People generally come to me for coaching because they want to improve an area of their life. Sometimes they know precisely what they want, but often they aren't totally clear, and that's why they need help figuring out exactly what's going on and then figuring out how we get them there. Instead of compartmentalizing and focusing solely on a specific problem or something they want, I look at their life as a whole and focus my attention on what is needed most. When we do that, when we take that thirty-thousand-foot view of our lives, we begin to uncover what's lacking on a more fundamental level. What is the deeper need to be fulfilled? Is it a sense of security? Purpose? Adventure? Love? Connection to others? Identifying the underlying need or desire will always help us more clearly understand what we need to do in order to better our life.

As you read this book, you'll see many examples of folks who thought they needed to focus on one area, but after a simple assessment—one that you'll also do in this chapter—they could see clearly that it was actually a different area that required taking action first. It's so important to start in this way so that you can get a specific vision of where to make some decisions to move forward.

If you've seen me on *Dr. Phil*, you read *Best Self*, or you follow me on social media, you know I love assessments. I'm a huge believer in them. Now, before you start rolling your eyes, gritting your teeth, and turning the page, hear me out. I know assessments get a bad rap. And I get it! It's always driven me nuts that every time I visit a doctor, I have to fill out the same monotonous, tedious twenty-page document. *The same forms!* Every single time I check in at the reception desk, they hand me that dreaded clipboard and an almost-out-of-ink pen, and I set about answering question after boring question about my health conditions.

The truth is, there's value in filling out those assessments. They help you and your physician understand the point from which you're starting. They define your baseline, what's going on with you currently, and what you're hoping to achieve. And that's what we want to achieve here—to define your starting point, and to discover where it is you want to improve. In this case, however, there's no one reviewing your answers except for *you*. You'll get to learn and discover so much about yourself by doing this exercise. (And by the way, if you're interested in seeing how other folks answered, or if you want to share your own answers, I encourage you to visit Coach Mike Bayer on Facebook to share with my community!)

We live our day-to-day lives within our own bodies, brains, and emotions, and we rarely take the time to step back and look at what is a "better" life for us. But how can we expect to have a better life if we don't even know what that looks like? And if it sounds complicated, it's really not. I think you'll find that once you start to drill down just a bit, discovering what it is that you *really* want is actually much easier than you might imagine.

Think of your life as one giant puzzle. The pieces are made up of all the different areas of your life. The specifics of those pieces will differ somewhat for all of us, but the key is to assess how we feel about each of them. The best way to know what we really want to change in our lives, or the areas that most need our attention, is to lay them all out and consider them objectively.

As you'll see, I've created a chart with the overarching areas of your life. There are blank lines that you will fill in as they apply to you. When you look at each category, first notice your immediate reaction to that category. Do you feel calm and peaceful when you look at some? Or do you notice yourself tensing up when you look at some areas? Or maybe even as if you've been sucker punched, because that area is particularly painful for you? You might even feel immediately as if you want to avoid the area altogether and not think about it. These instantaneous reactions are very telling and give us some great information about ourselves.

Then think about the specifics of that area of your life. Is that area causing issues for you? Is there something going on that's taking up a disproportionate amount of your time, causing you to worry, or creating stress for you? Is it causing you to feel as though your security or safety has been threatened? Or does that area bring you joy and help you feel fulfilled? Do you perhaps feel stuck in some areas, as if you've sort of stagnated within them? Take all of these things into consideration before the next step.

In case you're not sure what one of the areas means, or you need a little guidance on how best to rate them, here are some ideas to get you started:

- **FAMILY:** Depending on your situation, this could pertain to your given or biological family. Under this umbrella are your sibling and parental relationships, as well as grandparents, cousins, extended family.

- **FRIENDSHIPS:** This area is for all of your friendships. If you feel like you don't have as many friends as you'd like to, or so many that you feel you can't give all of them adequate attention, then you might rate this area lower. Or if one particular friendship is causing problems, that may also result in a lower rating.

- **ROMANTIC RELATIONSHIPS:** If you have a partner or spouse, this area pertains to that relationship. Or if you're dating, then this area is about your dating life.

- **PARENTING:** If you have a child/children, this is an area that can be tough to rate. Depending on how your kids are doing right now, you might feel like this area is under control, but as soon as something goes wrong, you might judge yourself harshly. Try to be as objective as possible.

- **EMPLOYMENT:** This applies to you if you are currently working. How do you feel about your job? Does it make you feel that you are making a worthy contribution to the world, or to the organization? Are you happy to go to work each day? Or does it feel like you're just punching a clock?

- **PHYSICAL HEALTH:** Your physical health is regarding how you feel. Are you in chronic pain? Are you suffering with health conditions that you haven't addressed? Do you take care of your body, or do you tend to ignore it?

- **EMOTIONAL HEALTH:** This realm includes your mental health. Are you struggling with anxiety, depression, or mood swings? Do you have trouble regulating your emotions? Do you have anger issues, or do you feel suffocated by worry? Alternatively, do you feel in control of your emotions, and that you are able to function well even under stress?

● **SPIRITUAL HEALTH:** Do you have a good connection with your own spirituality? This means different things for different people. When rating this area, think about how aligned you are with your spiritual beliefs on a day-to-day basis.

● **HOBBIES:** This might be an area you could easily gloss over, but consider in what ways you are exploring your passions. Are you actively learning about topics that interest you? Or spending time doing things simply because they light you up?

● **FINANCIAL HEALTH:** How do you feel about your finances? Are you often stressed out about money? Are you worried you haven't saved enough for your future? Or do you have a financial plan or budget that you adhere to in order to feel peaceful about your money matters?

KNOW WHERE YOU'RE GOING: IT'S ASSESSMENT TIME!

In the following "Life Assessment" chart, mark a box to rate each area on a scale of 1 to 5. If an area does not apply to your life, simply mark N/A. If one of them is creating negative energy in your life, you might mark a 1 or 2. If it's neutral—meaning, it's not problematic, but it could use some improvement—you might rate it at a 3. If it's operating well for you, you might choose a 4 or 5.

The next step is to ask ourselves whether we are motivated to make a change in a specific area right now. This is important because when we are experiencing stress or negativity in a particular area of life, sometimes our instinct is just to bury our head in the sand and ignore it. Only you can decide when the time is right for dealing with such issues. Now may not be that time. You may have other priorities that you need to tend to for the time being. We don't want to guilt ourselves into change; that isn't effective. Instead, let's focus on areas that you are motivated to change right now.

So, under the "Am I motivated to change it?" heading, write down your thoughts. Maybe you write, "Not for now, but soon" under some, or "Yes! I need to work on this urgently" under others. It's completely up to you. The idea here is just to complete the assessment so that you can have a clear vision of your current life landscape. Try not to get ahead of yourself and start thinking about how you're going to change it. For now, we just want to identify the areas of highest need. If there is an area of your life that isn't already listed in the chart, I encourage you to write it down and rate it accordingly in the blank spaces provided.

LIFE ASSESSMENT

AREA OF LIFE	N/A	RATING 1-5	AM I MOTIVATED TO CHANGE IT?
Family			
Friendships			
Romantic Relationships			
Parenting			
Employment			
Physical Health			

(continued)

AREA OF LIFE	N/A	RATING 1-5	AM I MOTIVATED TO CHANGE IT?
Emotional Health			
Spiritual Health			
Hobbies			
Financial Health			

THE HEART OF THE ISSUE

One of the most powerful reasons for using the life assessment is to make sure you are addressing the actual area in need. For instance, as I've mentioned, I've worked with people who say they really need to make more money, but when we unpack it a bit, the reality is that they are trying to solve emotional issues with money. As we work through and talk about those issues, that's when they discover that it's really about security, or safety. And not making money, or hitting financial hard times, can then activate a fear and make someone feel unsafe. So the most helpful thing to do is to investigate all the areas of life that make them feel unsafe. From that starting point, we can understand what it is we truly want instead of just focusing on that external thing that doesn't ever really resolve the feeling inside us.

Another example is someone who rates their romantic relationships as a 1 because they aren't in a relationship, but the question is, do they really want one? Is it truly important to them? If they spend time getting aligned with their authenticity, they can take a look at what they actually do want in their life.

Those are just a couple of ways in which we sometimes think we should be focusing on one area, but really it's a different area that first requires our attention. As you look at your chart, think about the heart of the issue for you, and let that be your starting point.

INTERPRETING YOUR ASSESSMENT

Even if you rated all areas of your life as a 1 and said they urgently need to change, I still encourage you to focus on one area right now—because one change, One Decision, can end up shifting all areas of your life. What I've found again and again is that once we begin to bring the most troublesome area of our lives back into stability, the other areas will often follow suit, or at least experience great improvements. Because all these puzzle pieces work together to create a whole, often making positive change in one area will directly impact another. And our successes can boost our confidence, helping us to start a bigger flow of positive change in our lives. In other words, we don't want to try to take everything on all at once. Instead, let's zero in.

Look at your "Am I motivated to change it?" column, and think about where you are naturally inclined to focus your attention. You could ask yourself, "If this area were to drastically improve, how would I feel?" in order to choose where to begin. What we don't want to do is to start thinking a lot about the actual obstacles ahead of us in a particular area, or sending ourselves messages about how hard it's going to be. We simply want to think about how much we will benefit from making positive changes in a given area of our lives.

Once you've narrowed it down to one area, write it here:

The area I want to focus on improving is:

_____

Now that you have a clear vision of which area of your life you want to focus on first, let's think about to what degree you want to create change in that area, as well as the type of change you're looking to achieve. Based on how you rated that area, and how much it's affecting your ability to love your life, you may need to bring about some extreme change, or you may just need to make simple shifts. To help you determine this, I'm going to introduce you to something I refer to as the REP Scale.

THE REP SCALE

Sometimes an area of your life feels completely out of sync with who you are, like you can't believe you ended up in this spot that just doesn't feel like "you" at all. If that's the case, don't worry. There is a path back to your authenticity, and we are going to discover it together.

On the other hand, you may just be feeling like you need to make some changes here and there, and your life will feel *so* much better. Here's the bottom line: there are degrees to which we might need to bring about change in our lives, and to help you discern to what degree you are seeking to change, I've created something called the REP Scale.

REINVENT
EVOLVE
PIVOT

Here's what each one means:

REINVENT:

- To reinvent is to overhaul. It is a significant shift, so big in fact that life looks completely different. You might be feeling like you need to completely change some or several aspects of your life that aren't working for you. Perhaps your physical health is suffering and it's affecting your quality of life. Or maybe your employment situation is causing you extreme stress, and you need to make a change. A reinvention might mean making a decision to start doing things completely differently than you have been so that you can start getting a completely different outcome.

- Some examples of reinventions include losing a significant amount of weight, going off to college, getting sober, divorcing a spouse. A reinvention is when we are starting fresh, starting over, and shifting so much that we come back as totally different from before. Often in life, we can get really stagnant, and it might require a reinvention to reconnect with your passion.

Evolve:

- When you think of evolve, think of it as *growing up* and *glowing up*. It means that it's time you evolve with the world around you so that as it gets upgraded, you upgrade yourself as well. To evolve means accepting your reality, embracing the change, and maturing.

- It could mean that you need to make health decisions because you're older and starting to have more health concerns. It could mean not going out to bars and clubs if you now have a job that requires early hours. It could be changing your hobbies so that you can shift to a more appropriate peer group.

Pivot:

- A pivot can create big change with just a small step in a new direction. For instance, you may make a decision that you'll no longer engage in gossip, or that you will spend less time on social media or dating apps. It could be that you won't point out a flaw in one of your loved ones' approaches to life. Maybe it's seeking new training to improve your career. Or if your parenting techniques don't seem to be working on your child now that he or she has reached a certain age, it might be time to try something new.

- Examples include finding new methods for physical fitness that resonate with you, taking a class to make you feel inspired in life, growing the vegetables you always wanted to in your garden, or joining an online dating site.

Where I am on the REP Scale for this area of my life:

_____

THE DECISION TO . . .

As you move through this book, you'll be thinking about specific authentic decisions you need to make that will move your life in a more positive direction. To that end, I'd like to share with you some critical decisions that I've seen countless people make. These are so common that most of us will come to a point in our lives when we need to make each and every one of these decisions. Here is that list:

- the decision to let go

- the decision to get into a relationship

- the decision to stand up for ourselves

- the decision to improve our mental health

- the decision to start living a spiritual life

- the decision to end a relationship

- the decision to no longer be friends with someone

- the decision to stop enabling someone

- the decision to forgive someone

- the decision to speak up

These decisions mean different things to all of us, and apply in countless ways. We all have the power to make these decisions in our lives and to act on them. Our decisions are 100 percent our own responsibility, and although that can feel daunting for some, it is also exhilarating to know that we have the freedom to choose to live the life we want. I mean, how exciting is it to know that you are completely autonomous; you can make any decision you want. Right now, you've decided to read this book. Every word on every page that you choose to read—that's your decision. The motivation underneath that decision is likely to improve your life in some way, to learn more about your own behavior, and to take your life into your own hands. That's a decision that is in your best interest!

As you move into the next part of this book, we will begin to look at the FORCEs that can either help keep us on track with who we are or have us feeling completely out of alignment. We all do these, and none of these are all or nothing; they're just a part of what gets in the way of our having a better life. We're about to do some deeper work, but when we shift how we think, we shift how we feel, and then we shift how we behave, and the FORCEs can help us do just that. With an open mind, a willing spirit, and a hopeful heart, let's boldly proceed!

PART 2

THE

FORCE

4

THE FORCE THAT DRIVES DECISIONS

As I touched on earlier, there is a pattern of thinking that drives our perception of life. Both in my personal experience and in my working with thousands of clients, I've found that it's that perception that ultimately dictates whether we will make a decision that leads us to a better life or make a decision that causes more stress, pressure, and anxiety. For the most part, anytime we have a perceived problem, we look at the problem through a certain lens. We've likely all met someone facing a situation that we perceive as awful, yet they are optimistic or solution focused. Or perhaps we are being positive and someone else is focused on the negative. These telltale characteristics are driven by something I refer to as their FORCE.

The FORCE is essentially the patterns that we fall into, the thing that is driving our behavior. For example, let's say you get cut off in traffic. Then you get really angry and drive aggressively. That energy flows right into the next meeting you have, or person you talk to. That anxiety or frustration is lurking in your mind, unresolved and festering. When this happens again and again, it's because there's a FORCE that's driving that pattern of thinking. You may get better at resolving it in the moment, but identifying the FORCE underneath your behavior is the key to changing your behavioral patterns.

FORCE is an acronym, and for each letter in it, there is a "negative" force, which has us focused only on the obstacles, and a "positive" one, which allows us to see all the opportunities before us. These FORCEs are as follows:

FORTUNE-TELLING	and	**F**ACT-FINDING
OVERGENERALIZING	and	**O**BJECTIVE THINKING
RIGID MINDSET	and	**R**ELAXED MINDSET
CONFUSED PURPOSE	and	**C**LARIFIED PURPOSE
EMOTIONAL REASONING	and	**E**VIDENCE-BASED REASONING

In the chapters that follow, you will learn all the ins and outs of how these FORCEs can drive our decisions, and either sabotage or support our efforts to reinvent, evolve, or pivot in our lives. They can put a whole lot of horsepower in our engine of change, or they can stall us out on our journey toward a better life. The decision is ours.

To help you see just how these FORCEs play out, I will be sharing the stories of real coaching clients of mine who have gotten stuck in the negative FORCE, but a quick switch in perspective allowed them to make decisions that made them happier, wealthier (at least in some cases), and more fulfilled in a very short amount of time. The only thing that changed was their FORCE, or how they looked at their problem, and then they were able to home in on their One Decision and ensure it was coming from their Best Self.

The "negative" FORCEs, or the ones that cause us to view everything life throws our way purely as an obstacle, are examples of something referred to as cognitive distortions in cognitive behavioral therapy. Distortions that we allow to progressively worsen can exaggerate symptoms of depression, anxiety, substance abuse, and other forms of fear. The FORCE is a representation of the cognitive distortions that form patterns that I believe play the biggest roles in our decision making, specifically. I've also included the positive flip side of each negative FORCE that will help us get out of the various forms of distorted thinking and back into reality.

Shifting from distorted thinking, or "obstacle" thinking, and into "opportunity" thinking requires preparation, truth, and logic. It also requires a certain amount of creativity, in that we have to get inspired enough to see the potential opportunities before us. Those attributes show up again and again in the opportunity column because they are at the heart of the FORCEs that can shift us out of the obstacle mindset.

OVERVIEW OF THE FORCE

Here is an overview of what each of these FORCEs means so that you have a general idea of what they are before we go into more depth in the upcoming chapters in part 2.

FORCE

FORTUNE-TELLING: NEGATIVE FORCE

Fortune-telling is when we guess what someone else will do or think, and it's when we assume we know how a situation is going to turn out. Unlike an educated guess, fortune-telling is guessing without the information, the facts. When we're predicting the future in this way, or making assumptions, we are making guesses based upon a *story*. Sometimes these guesses may be true, and other times they aren't true.

Examples include the following:

- when we predict a supervisor will respond a certain way about a promotion

- when we think we know how a friend will respond without asking

- when we assume we're going to fail a test before we've even taken it

● when we catastrophize, or envision the absolute worst-case scenario that could play out—a common and extreme example of fortune-telling

FACT-FINDING: POSITIVE FORCE

The opposite of fortune-telling—and the way out of this harmful pattern of thinking—is called fact-finding. Fact-finding is where we figure out exactly what the facts are in any given situation. Rather than guessing how the supervisor might react when we ask for a promotion, we put together all the facts, all of the logical reasons why we believe we've earned the promotion, and then we present those facts to the supervisor. Or, rather than assuming we are going to fail a difficult test, we study and prepare for it, and answer the questions to the best of our abilities, without predicting the outcome. By living in the facts, rather than fantasy, we can ensure that our decisions are educated ones, rather than ones based on a story we have created in our minds.

FORCE

OVERGENERALIZING: NEGATIVE FORCE

When we are overgeneralizing, we are arriving at conclusions based on one stand-alone incident. A simple example would be running over a nail on the way home from work one day and then thinking, "Man, I run over *every* nail on the road." That'd be an overgeneralization. Or we catch a cold and then proclaim, "I catch every germ I'm exposed to." If a student gets a poor grade on one paper and then concludes, "I am a horrible student. I should just quit school," that'd be overgeneralizing. Or if we're in one political party and sometimes describe the other political party as ignorant, self-serving, homophobic, or any other label; it's impossible that every single member of a political party can be described in such a way. Overgeneralizing is what occurs when someone labels all Muslims as terrorists or all Christians as fanatics. There's no curiosity in it; it doesn't require you to explore the matter at all.

OBJECTIVE THINKING: POSITIVE FORCE

On the other hand, objective thinking requires a totally open mind. And open-mindedness is where curiosity lives. It's where truth lives. It's where flexibility lives. When we are approaching life with an open mind, we are able to create new ideas, explore new belief systems, and adopt new ways of thinking. It's also where progressiveness resides. When we are thinking objectively, we can embrace and exemplify empathy and compassion toward one another because we are more able to see another person's perspective or point of view. The result is that we are more at peace with the world around us. It also allows us to experience more inner peace because we look at our own lives objectively and with an open mind. Instead of overgeneralizing, we give ourselves more grace, more room for error and learning.

FORCE

Rigid mindset: Negative force

When we are being rigid, we might adopt a "my way or the high-way" mentality. Or we might be a "right fighter," always seeking to have the last word and to "win" every argument that comes our way. When applied to our decision making, if we are too rigid, we leave ourselves no room to consider alternate ways of achieving something. We might think this is the way we've always done things, so it must be the right way. A rigid mindset often means being so caught up in what we believe is right that we sometimes miss what is in our best interest.

RELAXED MINDSET: POSITIVE FORCE

The opposite of rigid, a "relaxed" mindset means that we are calm, less tense, and more willing to take a deep breath and open our eyes to what is in our best interest. When we are relaxed, others around us sense that calm energy and feel heard and seen, rather than like they are being forced into a specific way of thinking or doing things. Rather than viewing life within a specific box we have created for it, we are willing to blur the lines and accept life on life's terms instead of trying to dictate how life should be. When we're coming at problems in our life, a relaxed point of view would have us asking, "Is it really going to matter five years from now?" and that's a great way to give us more perspective.

FORCE

Confused purpose: Negative force

When we are stuck inside a "confusion" mindset, we might feel helpless, have anxiety, and become overwhelmed. This FORCE often causes us to overthink situations that arise. We might feel paralyzed because of the overanalysis and unable to make a decision. This is also what's happening when we seek too many opinions, or opinions from people who are not well versed in the topic at hand, and we start to lose touch with our purpose and even our authenticity because of all the voices in our head. When we're talking about confusion, we aren't talking about understanding a subject in school and prepping for a test. We are talking about *why* we're doing what we're doing. People pleasing and co-dependency can arise out of a state of confusion, when we're doing something because we think it's going to make us feel better but it doesn't.

CLARIFIED PURPOSE: POSITIVE FORCE

Confusion can often exist where there is no purpose; therefore, the way we can overcome the FORCE of confusion is to clarify our purpose. This is where relying on your decision team (which we will get to in more detail later) is hugely helpful, because you're asking people who have specific experience or wisdom about the decision you are trying to make and who can help you realign with your purpose. Once you have purpose, you have clarity and you are no longer in a state of confusion. For example, if you find yourself confused about whether you should attend someone's party, you need to clarify your purpose in attending. Is it in your best interest to attend because you will feel great showing up for your friend, or because there will be great networking opportunities that could push your career forward? Perhaps your purpose in it is to catch up with old friends. But if you show up at the party and wonder why you're there, it's because you don't know your purpose in being there. When you're confused, it's important to ask what decision will align with your own purpose, your Best Self, and what you really want in your life.

FORCE

Emotional Reasoning: Negative Force

We've often heard the saying "feelings aren't facts," but when we are using emotional reasoning, we struggle with that notion. Feelings can be quite powerful, and convincing. When we are using emotional reasoning, we believe feelings *are* the facts. This is what's occurring when you think, "Yeah, but I *feel* this way, so that's what I'm going to do (or not do)." There's a difference between following your gut instincts and following your feelings, but being driven by emotional reasoning can cause us to confuse the two. Emotions are so unreliable and so fleeting. Allowing fear, anxiety, or depression to guide our decisions is faulty because it does not prioritize our best interests. If a feeling of depression is making you stay inside all day and not interact with people in your life, then you are missing out on opportunities and on your life. It may feel good in the immediate term to isolate, but that's not in your best interest. I never used to see myself as a public speaker because it didn't *feel* good. There was fear in it. Emotional reasoning is a core reason why people don't push themselves to be better.

EVIDENCE-BASED REASONING: POSITIVE FORCE

You may notice an overarching theme beginning to emerge: that the opportunity-focused, positive mindset is often looking at what is logical. And when it comes to overcoming the FORCE of emotional reasoning, evidence is king. Getting to the truth of the matter, rather than how the matter makes you feel, is what can set you free. It never feels good the first time we do anything that requires people's approval—by that I mean that someone is paying you for it, or rating you on it, or what have you. There's anxiety because you aren't that good yet. You can try your best, but you still won't be the best. Even the rookie who is the No. 1 draft pick doesn't crush it in his first game in the NBA. He'll never tell you the first professional game played was his best. And that's someone we would consider a superstar! With my fear of public speaking, I just had to do it—to take that contrary action. Once I did, I started to see evidence that I actually enjoyed public speaking and that it aligns with my own goals and with my Best Self.

NEGATIVE FORCE	POSITIVE FORCE
Fortune-Telling:	**Fact-Finding:**
• Guessing what someone else thinks or what they'll do. • Predicting how a situation will turn out. • Catastrophizing—assuming worst-case scenario. • Holding opinions based on a story we've created, rather than facts.	• Gathering logical evidence. • Asking someone what they think, rather than predicting. • Asking an expert on the topic. • Engaging in educated guesses, rather than story-based guesses.
Overgeneralizing:	**Objective Thinking:**
• Drawing conclusions based on one stand-alone incident. • Labeling entire groups of people based on one person or experience. • Labeling ourselves as a result of one event.	• Considering all aspects of yourself, someone else, or a situation, not just an isolated moment in time. • Being curious and flexible. • Exploring new beliefs, embracing new ideas, and adopting new ways of thinking. • Exhibiting empathy and compassion; better able to appreciate someone else's point of view.
Rigid Mindset:	**Relaxed Mindset:**
• Having a "my way or the highway" mentality. • Right fighting—needing to be right in every exchange/ have the last word. • Believing that the way you've always done things is the only way to do them.	• Taking a calm approach, willing to take a deep breath. • Taking time to make others feel heard and seen. • Accepting life on life's terms instead of trying to dictate life. • Willing to ask, "Is it going to matter five years from now?"

NEGATIVE FORCE	POSITIVE FORCE
Confused Purpose:	**Clarified Purpose:**
• Overthinking situations to the point of feeling helpless, overwhelmed.	• Asking ourselves about the reason we're making a decision one way or another.
• Out of indecision, getting stuck in inaction.	• Realizing that some decisions are not about our "life's purpose" and that we might just have a role to play in certain situations.
• Seeking too many opinions, and losing touch with gut instincts.	
• Potentially becoming co-dependent.	• Understanding/discovering our purpose in any situation.
• People pleasing.	• Working with a decision team to help realign with your purpose.
Emotional Reasoning:	**Evidence-Based Reasoning:**
• Believing our feelings are facts.	• Getting to the truth of the matter.
• Making decisions based on how we feel.	• Making decisions based on the evidence, and not on a feeling.
• Not pushing ourselves to be better, because it doesn't always *feel* good.	• Pushing out of comfort zone in order to cultivate new skills.

WHICH FORCE WILL YOU CHOOSE?

I believe that the vast majority of problems we face are only problems because we *perceive* them as obstacles instead of opportunities. It's totally normal to look at obstacles in that negative light, by the way. To attach meaning to problems is natural. It's our brain's way of protecting us, really. We've experienced trouble in the past, we recognize a familiar roadblock, and it makes sense that we'd look at it in the same way. Our brain is basically saying, "Watch out! Avoid! We've been here before, and it does not end well!" But this is tricky, because we can't always assume that a new obstacle is the same one we've experienced in the past. We've got to look at it in the present context, with clear eyes.

How exactly do we do that? In the chapters that follow, I'm going to show you. Together, we are going to take a close look at some of the inner workings of your subconscious mind to find out how your brain has been hyper-focused on the obstacle to the point of completely missing the opportunity right in front of you. It's like a form of tunnel vision we all suffer from, so we're just going to get out of that tunnel and into the light.

It all comes down to what FORCEs are driving you. If you've unwittingly allowed the negative FORCEs to drive your decision making, then it's time to flip the script and choose positive FORCEs instead!

DECISION MAKING WHEN IN RECOVERY

Many people I have worked with who are in recovery from drugs, alcohol, food, gambling, PTSD, and so on report that when they got sober, their emotional capacity remained where it was when they started using drugs or alcohol. That can have a significant impact on their decision making, particularly if they started using substances at a young age. This is yet another reason why it's so useful to get a grasp on our own individual decision-making styles and strategies so that we can then adjust them to be in our own best interest.

ROLE OF THE BOOGEYMAN

The fears we had while growing up will often manifest themselves in our life today and influence the FORCEs that end up driving us. Without realizing it, we can often surrender control of life to those persistent fears—which I refer to as the Boogeyman. Left unchecked, the Boogeyman will steer us toward the negative FORCEs, and thus toward self-sabotage. We want to do whatever we can to keep that from happening, and I've found that the best way to avoid it is simply to bring awareness to our own specific Boogeyman.

Typically, whatever we were afraid of growing up is also what we're afraid of when we're adults. The Boogeyman is driven by fear, which is often referred to as **f**alse **e**vidence **a**ppearing **r**eal. For example, if we were a kid on the playground and we really struggled to be liked by our peers, that may still be a struggle we feel when we're grown-up. The Boogeyman can comprise events that happened in our early life that still haunt us today. For some, it might be a fear of abandonment, because Mom or Dad left the family. For others, if they were emotionally or sexually abused growing up, they're not going to feel safe in a lot of settings unless they are able to heal some of those past events. If someone grew up in an alcoholic family, they're typically going to get their self-worth through taking care of others, but that quality is a result of the caretaking they felt they had to do when their parent or parents were drinking. Whatever we experience as a child, especially any level of trauma, can turn into a Boogeyman that we carry with us throughout our lives. Here are some beliefs the Boogeyman can cause you to form at a young age, which can take root in your psyche and grow over time:

- You're not good enough.

- If people really got to know you, they wouldn't love you.

- You're not safe.

- You can't trust people.

- You are a fraud.

- You have to impress people.

- You have to keep secrets.

- You can't get too close to people, because they will leave you.

If beliefs like these are growing bigger in your own mind, becoming intolerable, or creating anxiety, then it might be time to ask for help so you can heal from them. These are not at all uncommon; many people go through their entire lives with a Boogeyman. The great news is that there are lots of modalities that can be extremely helpful in healing the hurts and making the Boogeyman disappear once and for all. You might discover your own method of healing, and if you feel your Boogeyman dissipating as you gain power over him, then what you're doing is likely working. Either way, it begins with awareness, so as you work your way through these FORCE chapters, be alert to any signs that you might have a Boogeyman trying to take the controls in your life.

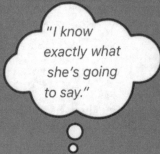

5

Force

FORTUNE-TELLING OR FACT-FINDING

Take a look at these thought bubbles. Do any of these sound familiar? Have you ever convinced yourself you know exactly how events are going to play out and then based your decisions and actions on that story you're telling yourself? If your answer is yes, don't feel bad—we all do this! It's called fortune-telling and it's incredibly common. It can originate from our past experiences, or even from our Boogeyman, but one thing is for sure: fortune-telling does not come from our Best Self, and it does not lead us to authentic decisions. The truth is, we cannot predict what's ahead on the road to reinventing ourselves, evolving with the world around us, or pivoting to create a better life. That's why we want to keep ourselves firmly rooted in the facts. Fact-finding is the FORCE that opposes fortune-telling, and it can snap us right out of that fortune-telling haze. It can sharpen up our focus and help us make clearheaded decisions based on our Best Self, instead of ones based on fictional stories invented out of fear.

One of my friends, Mike, is a personal trainer at an elite gym, and he also has his own personal training business. He is often referred to as Coach Quads (his Instagram handle is @coachquads) because he's well-known for his gigantic legs. I mean, they are enormous. But he's much more than just a personal trainer with impressive musculature. Mike is thoughtful, focused, and reliable; he would never take advantage of anyone. And he just so happens to be one of the best personal trainers out there. And so it might surprise you to know that he sometimes sells himself short; it certainly surprised me when we sat down for a coaching session and it became clear that he was engaging in fortune-telling and basing his career decisions on an unfounded story he was telling himself. Essentially, he believes he can predict what someone is going to say before they even say it. Here's his story.

Mike is not just a fantastic personal trainer whose clients have seen massive success in getting into good physical shape. He also has a finely tuned skill set that allows him to train people who have severe and complex mental health issues. Therefore, people who have been struggling through suicidal thoughts and attempts, battling severe depression or anxiety, who can barely get out of bed in the morning, much less get in an hour of cardio, have improved their lives by leaps and bounds by working with Mike. Keep in mind—we are in Los Angeles, where concierge personal training and other services are the "norm" and people are used to paying more here than perhaps in other regions for these types of services. And with all that Mike has to offer, he could pretty much charge whatever he wants. However, he has always been extremely hesitant to change his rates at all. When we'd discussed it previously, he'd told me that the neighborhood he'd grown up in had a specific viewpoint on people who left the neighborhood and went elsewhere to become successful. He had referred to it as a "who do you think you are?" mentality. I thought we'd start there in our recent conversation.

"So, people have a 'who do you think you are?' mentality where you grew up?" I asked.

He replied, "Yeah, like 'Who do you think you are, becoming a celebrity trainer, charging that rate for an hour? That's what I make for an entire day!'" he said, smiling broadly.

"Right. I would refer to those voices from your family and the neighborhood as your Boogeyman. Who do you still hang out with from back home?"

Shaking his head, he said, "No one, actually. It's become this fictitious 'they' in my mind, really. I even talk to my clients about that 'they' voice in their heads, those who are somehow keeping them down, or making them think they can't accomplish more. It's all this subconscious BS that we tell ourselves."

"So, this 'who do you think you are?' label you are putting on yourself—what could be a loving message to send yourself instead?" I asked.

"You deserve it, you can do it," he said right away.

"Okay, and what do you think you're so scared of when it comes to increasing your rates?" I asked.

"I don't know that I'm *afraid* of anything. It's more this internal dialogue that holds me back than actual fear," he said.

"Let's say you were going to increase your rates with someone from the facility who wanted to become a private client. Walk me through how that conversation would go. They call you and say, 'Mike, I'd really like to continue training with you.' You then say . . .'"

"I would mention how well they've done in the time we've already worked together. I'm a positive person and give positive feedback. We'd then discuss where we would train, do they have a facility, and all that," he said.

"When does money come up?" I asked.

"Probably right after that."

"How do you feel when they ask you that?"

"Nervous," he said.

"You get anxiety?"

"Yeah, and I tend to get anxiety around money," he replied.

"Okay, but let's get granular. A client you've been working with at their psychiatric facility who is used to paying you a certain amount wants to become a private client. They're not new to the costs of these types of services. In fact, you're currently charging half of the amount they're used to paying for personal training at the facility. So why do you essentially feel the need to cut that rate in half?"

"My thought process is they would definitely become my client if I give them a rate that is the cheapest it could be."

"So they're paying tens of thousands of dollars per month for psychiatric care, and they're *really* concerned about the hundred-dollar discount for a personal training session? Don't you think you're connecting dots that don't really exist? And fortune-telling how they would react?" I asked, in jest.

He laughed and replied, "I'm finding this hysterical. It's my blue-collar, ingrained mindset thinking it's a lot of money to spend on this type of service."

"On you! That type of service being you. They can spend that type of money for the same service but in a gym. But with you, they're working out at home, which is more convenient for them, and they may even need *more* TLC in the process, like you texting them three times a week. Those clients in particular really benefit from that support; they want to continue because they really enjoy working with you and they trust you in that. But you're fortune-telling that they won't pay you what you're worth. The opposite of fortune-telling is fact-finding. So I want us to look at the facts." I continued, "First, where do you think it hurts you not to be charging more?"

"I mean, obviously it hurts me financially. I could be working the same amount and be making more money or I could cut my hours and have more family time."

"And money is a stressor for you, right?"

"Correct. And not spending time with my family because I'm working is also a stressor for me. Right now, I set it up so that I get at least a quarter of a day with my son. Because there are times when I don't see him the whole entire day."

"So, you could have a menu of what you offer. One menu item could be training, but then you could offer to check in with them three times a week to make sure they're going on morning walks, sticking to their nutrition, and they're on the plan. Would people not *want* more of you?"

Thinking about this, he said, "Probably. Probably. And I also feel like as a trainer I'm always conscious that I'm not overpowering in a way. Not pushing too much. Whereas I probably should do that a little bit more, and just offer it. Then it's up to them."

"It sounds like you're terrified of the rejection," I said.

"Yes. That's everything. That's my entire life, is fear of rejection."

"Right. And it sounds like you're terrified of someone saying to you, 'Why are you so expensive?' So you're just predicting the worst-case scenario, and not even approaching the issue at all." That's when I noticed a big smile spreading on his face. "Are you willing to set the new price based on this conversation? Because you're smiling," I said.

He laughed and said, "Yes. Yes. I see it. And what makes me laugh about it is I also see how ridiculous it is! I see people do it on the fitness side all the time. This whole song and dance they'll give me of why they can't do it, why they can't be successful at X, Y, and Z. I guess you'd say they're fortune-telling too. I don't do that when it comes to fitness, but I see now that I'm doing it when it comes to money."

"So, let's say now you're charging twice your current rate per hour to go to someone's house and train them. Which, by the way, is also your time, it's your travel, energy, gas, and it's the luxury of having someone come to their home to train. I mean, the reality is that going just eight miles in Los Angeles can take up to an hour and a half, so that's three hours of travel plus an hour of training your client. You want to spend more time with your six-year-old son, you're willing to give more energy to clients, so if you take on fewer clients, you can provide a better service, you'll be fresher, more motivated, and it gives you more wiggle room. So, let's try this out. Tell me why do you deserve to charge that new rate?"

"I have twenty-two-plus years of experience. That's one. And I would say the last seventeen of that, give or take, have been working also in a mental health capacity."

"Wow, so for seventeen years you've been working with people who are struggling with clinical depression and acute disorders and you feel very comfortable working with that population, which is very unique and very different. You've worked with clinical teams."

Nodding his head, he said, "Yes. And that experience has trickled in across the board to all my clients. So I don't just operate in that capacity at a facility. I now take into account all aspects of someone's life. I treat every session as an opportunity to either improve something or heal or nuance something. I'm always adjusting the workouts, ramping up the workouts. I've been told by clients I have an extremely good intuition as to what they need in the moment."

"Got it. So, let's say someone calls you and says, 'Hey, I'd like to train with you. What do you cost?' You tell them the new rate. And let's just play it out for worst case. Let's say their reaction is 'Oh my gosh, I could get my hair dyed *and* a perm for that much! Why so much?'"

Calmly and with conviction, he replied, "I have twenty-two years' experience in the business. I have a ton of that experience in not only a training capacity but in a mental health care capacity, so you're getting a nuanced style of training that's more suited to developing a better lifestyle pattern than just working you out."

I said, "You presented them with the *facts*. How does that feel saying that?"

"It feels good. Yeah, it does," he said, his confidence rising.

"It feels true," I said.

"Yeah, it does. I do have a bit of that 'who do you think you are?' mindset, so I'm still worried I'm going to seem fraudulent."

"I think the opportunity here is to turn that 'who do you think you are?' into 'I know who I am!' or like 'I'll tell you who I am! I'm the guy who's been doing this for twenty-two years. I'm the guy who has over seventeen years working with people in mental health, and I'm the guy that's going to help you achieve your goals if you dig in with me. I will give you a higher and more specialized level of service and your results will show that. *That's* who I think I am.' Because that's who you are. Right?"

"Right," he said.

"And some of these clients actually need more nuanced support, so there's also an opportunity for you to provide them with more accountability. And call that the accountability program. It's not forcing on anyone. It's an option that really helps people. I like when someone says to me, 'Here's what I can do that can be helpful for you, or not.' It's providing a service that someone needs that's going to help them achieve their goals. So, really, it's an opportunity for you and for your clients."

"Yes, that's right," he said.

"Okay. What did you take away from this?"

"That I am deserving of a higher rate. And that I have allowed this kind of subconscious thinking to override in a default setting, like I'm not even consciously doing it. I hit this emotional panic and I start undercutting myself because I'm afraid of what they'll say. And it's completely unjustified. I need to be more confident by looking at the facts—which are my experience and my ability."

"You were perceiving things in a way that it was causing you to not see your worth and how deserving you are. You were existing in the obstacle of it, and fortune-telling how it was going to play out. Now that you're living in the facts, and seeing the opportunities, you made your decision about what to do next. And we have a plan where you're going to call me and we'll talk through how it goes and perhaps you can speak to your wife about it because she's a support system for you. She'll help encourage you, right?"

"Yeah!"

"She'll probably say, 'Mike is saying all the things I've been saying!' Right?"

"Yes, for sure."

I firmly believe that you get what you pay for and you charge what you're worth. To become an expert in any industry, you have to know the facts of being in that industry. A twenty-one-year-old personal trainer who just got out of college has not yet had enough training to treat a niche population. But Mike had put in years of dedication to his unique skills; he'd created a hybrid of life coaching and personal training in which the client benefits greatly. You may be in a service industry and you might have been in it for a long time, and what people are paying for is your years of honed expertise.

Mike did get a call from a potential client just a couple days later, and he did charge a new rate. The client didn't bat an eye. Mike had been fortune-telling what people might say if he charged this higher rate, and it had kept him trapped for years, really. But once he started fact-finding, laying it all out on the table, he could easily see that he was perfectly justified in charging a higher rate.

In any kind of service-based business, people often say they don't like to talk about their rates or fees. That can come from lack of self-confidence, from not believing in one's own value, but ultimately, at its core, it usually boils down to a fear of rejection.

Fortune-Telling:

- Guessing what someone else thinks or what they'll do.
- Predicting how a situation will turn out.
- Catastrophizing—assuming the worst-case scenario.
- Holding opinions based on a story we've created, rather than facts.

Fact-Finding:

- Gathering logical evidence.
- Asking someone what they think, rather than predicting.
- Asking an expert on the topic.
- Engaging in educated guesses, rather than story-based guesses.

WHAT IS FORTUNE-TELLING?

Fortune-telling is, fundamentally, acting out of your fear. It is guessing without the information. When we're predicting the future in this way, or making assumptions, we are making guesses based upon a *story*. Sometimes these guesses may be true, and other times they aren't true at all. Here are some examples of fortune-telling:

- guessing what someone else thinks

- guessing how someone else will feel

- guessing what someone else will do

- predicting how a situation will turn out

- catastrophizing—assuming the worst-case scenario

- holding opinions based on a story we've created, rather than facts

Fortune-telling removes the element of curiosity because it sends your mind to a specific expected result. But life is so unpredictable; we cannot possibly know every variable at play in any given situation, so it's unlikely that we can predict most things with much accuracy. Just as we wouldn't make decisions based on a crystal ball, leaning on fortune-telling in order to make decisions in our lives can be dangerous.

There are, on the other hand, many things we can guess that are true based on repeated successes. For instance, if someone drops an object, I can predict it's going to hit the floor because of an invisible force called gravity. What I *can't* predict is whether someone is going to drop something in the first place. There are, of course, times when predicting the future to some degree is a necessary skill, but I don't define this as fortune-telling. Instead, that's making an educated prediction. Like when a stoplight turns green, we can make an educated guess that cars will be coming, and we should wait until it turns red before walking across the road. You can see the difference: an educated guess can keep you safe because it is based in actual fact, rather than irrational fear.

The main reason we engage in fortune-telling is that we think it will protect us from rejection.

It might serve to prevent us from a potentially heated conversation, or from feeling disappointed, or from anxiety. But it's driven by fear, or by avoidance. We might predict that someone won't care about a certain topic, but we didn't even ask. We often *think* we have enough facts to make an assumption, but in reality we haven't fully explored the issue. Upon investigation, it often turns out that those "facts" we have in our mind are pure fiction.

FORTUNE-TELLING IN RELATIONSHIPS

As we get to know people in our lives, we begin to understand what type of behavior or situation may rub them the wrong way, and the best ways to approach them in order to get the desired result. This is actually an important life skill; it is part of intimacy and of really getting to know someone. It is also *very* different from fortune-telling. When we tailor our delivery of certain information to someone because we know them well, that's not fortune-telling.

Fortune-telling is when we believe that we can actually predict exactly how someone is going to react, or what they're going to do, think, or say, and thus avoid approaching the topic. Ultimately, we are not responsible for other people's feelings. But we can discover ways of communicating with them such that they are more likely to positively receive the message.

WHAT'S THE POSITIVE FORCE TO USE INSTEAD?

When we do find ourselves in a pattern of fortune-telling, we can always choose to use the positive FORCE of *fact-finding* instead. By living in the facts, rather than stories we have created in our heads, we can ensure that our decisions are educated ones. Furthermore, when we are fact-finding, we are more able to make decisions that are in our best interest and coming from our Best Self, rather than from a place of fear.

When we've been fortune-telling about someone or something specific, an important place to start is to ask ourselves whether it matters. For instance, if you're fortune-telling that someone doesn't like you, they may not like you! But the bigger question is, are you okay with that? I've learned in my own life that some people don't like me for whatever reason. And I'm not the only person they dislike in their life! I have no control over that, nor do I wish to have any. So, the *fact* in all of this is that if someone does not like you, you can be totally okay with it. They may be reacting to you for a reason that has to do with their upbringing, or some other experience in their own life, meaning it doesn't even have anything to do with you.

When we try to predict how a situation is going to play out, but we don't have any solid, reliable, and verifiable evidence to back our prediction, we just spin our wheels, stress ourselves out, and miss out on opportunities. We also stagnate our decision making because we whip ourselves into a fear frenzy. But when we're in the midst of a full-on fortune-telling takeover, it can be difficult to realize that's what's happening. Here are some other ways in which people fall prey to fortune-telling, which I share so that you can more easily spot this behavior in your own life and choose to focus on the facts instead.

Perhaps there's a big test, performance, or event coming up. Maybe you've struggled in the past with a similar task, so the assumption is that this time will be a struggle too. Regardless of how much time, effort, and energy you've put into preparing, there's a nagging feeling that it will not go well.

This is where this FORCE can become particularly dangerous because we run the risk of creating a self-fulfilling prophecy. If we tell ourselves enough that we're going to fail at something, then we could very well fail because we told our brain to do so! Our brain will do what we tell it to, so if we wire it for failure, that's just what will happen. And it's hardly motivating to work hard and prepare, study, or practice for something if we "know" we are going to fail. Fortune-telling our own failure is a form of self-sabotage. Also, when we're actively predicting that we're going to fail, we just feel shitty! And when we feel shitty, we don't make decisions that align with our Best Self. If we rely on fact-finding, however, we can look at how well prepared we are, examples where we've succeeded in the past. We can look at other moments where we have struggled in the past too, but we now acknowledge that we have the power to change it this time around, and other truths that factor into the situation.

Another way this shows up is when we conclude that someone is reacting negatively to us or judging us. Given no concrete evidence, we just conjure up a belief that they think poorly of us, or are silently criticizing us. Even though the person is most likely in their own world and not even thinking about us (who knows—maybe they're just constipated!), this can be such a powerful force that we create an entire narrative about how they "hate" us. Yikes! It's easy to see how this can lead down a negative path and toward false conclusions. I notice this a lot when people have been judged harshly by others or, worse, bullied by someone in the past. Bullying can leave lasting marks on our psyche, and the instinct is to protect ourselves from ever being bullied again. It's understand-able, of course, but if we allow that past experience to color our current experience, we are just giving our power away to the bully. It does not serve us to live a life of indecision, or to make decisions based on an irrelevant experience. Instead, we need to do every-thing we can to operate within the present and within the facts.

The truth is, we are not mind readers. We cannot know what someone else is thinking unless they tell us. So, if it's really im-portant that we know what a person thinks about something, then we have to ask them. But I would also say, if we are putting so much weight on what others think of us, and potentially allowing that to sway our decisions one way or another, that could be a sign that our priorities are out of order. If we're stressing out about how someone else perceives us, it's best to opt instead to focus on the facts as they relate to our Best Self. We can always return to the list of your own best attributes, as we wrote out in *Best Self*, and continue our decision making based on those, rather than on the opinions of others.

MAKING IT A TREASURE HUNT

A friend and I had been discussing ways in which she often fell into a pattern of fortune-telling in her life, and when she started really laying out the facts next to her predictions, she was so sur-prised how far afield she'd strayed. She quickly discovered that she'd been fortune-telling in many areas of her life and was really excited to reverse that habit.

She has a five-year-old son, and one night, over dinner, he said, "Mom, I have a question, but I know you're going to say no." Bingo. She recognized immediately what was going on. These habits start at an early age!

Armed with her new knowledge, she replied, "Before you ask the question, I have one for you. Do you know what fortune-telling means?" He shook his head no. "Well, fortune-telling is when you think you know exactly what the other person is going to say before you even ask them the question. Does that sound familiar?"

He laughed and said, "Yes! But I really do know!"

She said, "Okay. What's your question?"

"Can we go swimming tomorrow?" he asked, almost downtrodden, knowing for sure she was going to say no way.

She replied, "Why do you think I'm going to say no?"

He said, "Because you *always* say no."

"If I always said no to swimming, then how is it possible that we've ever gone swimming in your entire life?" she retorted.

He thought about this. "Well, you don't *always* say no. But you're going to this time."

She said, "Before I answer your question, let's play a little game. You know how you love to go on treasure hunts and find coins that people dropped outside?" He nodded emphatically. Treasure hunting was his favorite pastime, second only to swimming. "Okay. Right now, I want you to think about facts as treasure. We're going to go on a fact-finding treasure hunt. Okay?"

A little unsure, but willing to play along, he said, "Okay."

"What is a fact about days that we go swimming?"

He thought about this, and then his eyes lit up and he said, "They're warm!"

"Right!" she said. "We go swimming on warm days. What's another fact about days we go swimming?"

He said, "They're sunny! No rain!"

She smiled and replied, "Exactly! We go swimming on warm, sunny days. How can we find out if it will be warm and sunny tomorrow?"

He pointed at her phone and said, "Check the weather!"

"Good plan! We can hunt for facts on the weather app. Let's see"—she checked her phone—"it looks like it's going to be pretty warm and sunny tomorrow. So ask me your question again."

"Can we go swimming tomorrow?" he asked, a little more hopeful.

"Yes!" she replied. He clapped and did a little dance in his seat.

She told me that following that conversation her son would stop himself anytime he was about to predict what she was going to say, and instead they would go "hunting for facts" together. What a great way to get started off in life—choosing to let the facts take precedence over our past experiences or imagined predictions.

THE POSITIVE AND NEGATIVE *F* FORCES IN YOUR OWN DECISION MAKING

We all choose not to do certain things because we are afraid they won't work out in our favor. For some people, it's asking for a raise.

In the above story, it was predicting a parent's response. For some, it's avoiding relationships out of a fear of being rejected. For whatever area of life that you're currently looking to improve, let's investigate and find out if you might be fortune-telling in that area.

EXERCISE

How might you be currently fortune-telling in your life? Let's find out.

Your first step is to look at the area of your life that you assessed in chapter 2 as the area you most want to improve. Or, if there's something more urgent going on in your life today that you need to address, let's look at that. Write it down here:

_____

_____

_____

_____

_____

_____

Next, take a look at this chart of fortune-telling examples from people I've worked with, just to help you see how it can play out in our lives. And you'll see, in the right column, I list the facts of the situation. Looking at these side by side can help you see the stark difference in these two mindsets.

FORTUNE-TELLING	FACT-FINDING
There's no work available for my skill set.	There are hundreds of thousands of job openings every single day in the United States, no matter what's happening in the economy.
The economy will never rebound.	The economy has rebounded before.
I'm too old; no one would hire me.	People my age have been hired in the past.
I'll never have as much fun sober.	There are a lot of sober people who say they have more fun now.
I'll never find love.	People fall in love all the time, at all different ages and life stages.
I can't improve my health without sacrificing too much of my time.	I can't know until I try, and the fact is, plenty of healthy habits take no time at all.

Now look at this list, and see where you may be making excuses that are keeping you from having what you really want in your life. Write them in the "My Own Fortune-Telling" column. Then write out the facts in the "My Fact-Finding" column.

MY OWN FORTUNE-TELLING	MY FACT-FINDING

What is a decision to make based upon those facts that you discovered? This exercise helps to cognitively clarify what the truth is for you. In making decisions, we do not want to operate from fear. We want to operate from within the facts. So, what is a fact-based decision you could make? Or are you at peace with things as they are? Write your answer here:

_____

_____

_____

_____

Finally, let's think about the common reasons why we engage in fortune-telling. Are you fortune-telling out of

Fear? If so, explain. _____

_____

Avoidance? If so, explain. _____

_____

Distraction? If so, explain. _____

_____

FACT-FINDING WITH BRAD

I recently worked with Brad, who had been working at the same company for quite some time, and he was really ready to make a change. But he was absolutely paralyzed. He knew for sure that he wanted to leave, and his reasons for going all made sense, but he was so convinced his employer was going to "screw him over" that he couldn't budge. I remember him pacing back and forth, just panicked over how terrible it was going to be for him and trying to strategize how he was going to handle it when they dropped the hammer. He said things like "They're going to blackball me, I know it." Indeed, the main reason he had sought my assistance as his thinking partner was so that I could help him plan for what to do once the company took action against him. He was preparing for something that might possibly never occur.

When I asked him what evidence he had for predicting they would react in this way, and try to hurt his chances of landing another job, he didn't have anything substantial. The most information he had was rumors of another employee who left, and the company refused to give that person a recommendation. But when we really got into the details, that was a totally different circumstance and not comparable to Brad's situation. That particular employee had been there for only a short time, he had lied on his résumé, and he had even been reported to HR on multiple incidents. So, that "evidence" Brad was using to prove his prediction was not valid.

You see, Brad had been fortune-telling what his employer was going to do in reaction to his leaving, but when we started to do the opposite, which is fact-finding, it quickly became clear that there was no basis for his fortune-telling. His predictions were based in fear, not in *fact*.

After we dissected the situation, he realized two things: first, that his fortune-telling was not serving him. He also saw that the obstacle he thought he'd be facing (that his company was going to blackball him) was not, in fact, *real*. After that realization, Brad calmed down considerably because he was now operating from a place of reason and logic, rather than fortune-telling and fiction. He made the decision to hand in his resignation. Once he did, he wasn't sitting around waiting for bad news or feeling anxious about the possible outcome. He had made his decision, and he stopped his impulse to engage in fortune-telling by returning to the facts at hand. This resulted in a feeling of peace about his decision.

In that same week, the company he was leaving sent a glowing recommendation to his new potential employer and offered him a generous severance package. They even still conduct business with him to this day; they have a very strong working relationship. It was truly the best possible outcome, and one that hadn't even occurred to him as a possibility when we'd first started talking, because he'd been so caught up in the ugly cycle of fortune-telling. The more he thought about it, the more he had believed the narrative he'd created and he was totally blind to the positive possibilities. It took a fact-finding expedition to get him out of that headspace and into logical reasoning.

FACT-FORWARD DECISION MAKING

As we continue onward, let's resolve to stay grounded in the facts so that we can make Best Self decisions toward a better life. Our desire to hark back to what's occurred in the past rather than remain in the present can be powerful, so let's just stay alert and aware. When we fortune-tell, we create more anxiety in our own lives and then make decisions that do not lead us to a better life. No one can predict the future. But what we can do is focus on the truth instead of a false reality so that we can make decisions from our Best Self. When in doubt, let the facts be your guide.

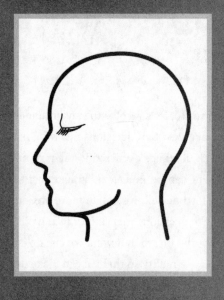

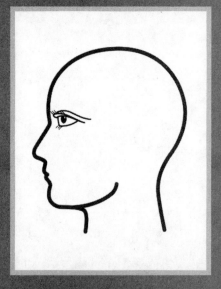

6

FORCE
OVERGENERALIZING OR OBJECTIVE THINKING

When we are overgeneralizing, we are "drawing a conclusion or making a statement about something that is more general than is justified by the available evidence." This FORCE can impact the way we think about life, about obstacles that arise, and even about ourselves and our capabilities. It is a way of thinking that is not coming from our Best Self, because it severely limits our view, and it can trick us into making decisions that don't come from our Best Self.

In the images at the beginning of the chapter, you see one person with their eyes closed and one with eyes open. The eyes-closed image connotes the concept of closed-mindedness, meaning we aren't considering the whole picture and instead just closing our eyes. We believe we already have all the information we need.

Whereas when our eyes are wide open, we are seeing the whole picture and making an authentic decision within it.

The easiest way to grasp overgeneralizing is to consider how people in one political party talk about people in the opposing party. There is a lot of labeling that goes on, and labeling is a form of overgeneralizing. A die-hard conservative might say that "all liberals are socialists who should move to another country and are unpatriotic," which, of course, cannot be true. He or she might base that opinion upon the words or actions of one particular liberal politician, but it is not accurate to apply that label to *all* liberals. On the other hand, a staunch Democrat might say of Republicans that they "are all homophobic, environment-hating jerks," which, again, is overreaching and impossible to be true of an entire group of people.

Objective thinking is the antidote, if you will, to overgeneralizing. When we're being objective, we aren't generalizing about something and drawing on old beliefs or even popular beliefs. We are looking at an obstacle for what it is, rather than applying flawed logic to the situation. Especially when it comes to how we view ourselves, objective thinking can help us easily get grounded in our authenticity.

I believe one of the times that we are the most susceptible to any of the negative FORCEs is when we are taking on something new. When we're first starting out in a new job, for instance, we want to show up as our Best Self, we want our co-workers and managers to like us, and we want to crush it in our new position. But if we experience adversity—someone doesn't seem to like us right off the bat, or we screw up on a task—we might start to think maybe we're no good or this isn't the right job. That's what the overgeneralizing FORCE can look like: we judge ourselves or entire experiences on isolated incidents. But imagine if we judged every job on a couple of isolated incidents; we might never stay in any position for more than a few days!

I've found that parents often tend to overgeneralize about themselves and their parenting abilities. Kelly, a colleague of mine, recently shared that she has almost a constant internal struggle with this phenomenon. She said, "I read parenting books and stay up with the latest research, and one of the biggest things I've taken away is that I should avoid yelling at my son. I've read the research, and I know that yelling can be detrimental. And so, I end up putting a lot of pressure on myself. Like, a *ton* of pressure. Sometimes I feel like I'll be crushed under it. But I just really do not want to be that yelling, screaming, crazy mom that goes 'nuclear' over the littlest thing. Despite that, if I've had a long day at work, or I'm overwrought for some other reason, and my son pitches a fit about brushing his teeth, or is on a nonstop whining loop, I'll huff, I'll puff, and then I'll blow my top and just start yelling commands. I'm seeing red at that point, and even though I know damn well I need to chill out, it's just so hard to stop once I get going."

Before she could continue, I asked, "What does that sound like?"

With a deep sigh, she replied, "Are you sure you want to hear?" I nodded, and she said, "Something like this," and she took a big breath and closed her eyes, and when she opened them, they had this wild look, and she mock yelled, " 'Matthew Stephen Jones, I swear to God, you had better cut out this behavior and start listening to me right this very minute or you will get no TV for a week!' "

I raised my eyebrows, smiled, and said, "Intense, yeah?"

She shook it off a bit and said, "Yeah. And that's nothin'. You have no idea. I'm so ashamed that I let myself do that. It's like I indulge in the anger, frustration, and exhaustion and I just let it all out like lava bursting from a volcano. It's awful."

"And so, when you think about these incidents after the fact, how does it make you feel?"

"Well, that's the thing. For a while, I was judging myself so harshly. I started believing that I'm just a terrible mom. Like, the worst mom in the history of the world. But what I found was that the more I was telling myself I was a terrible mom, the more I was actually yelling at him. It was this ugly cycle. So I started to think about it in terms of how often it happened versus how often my son and I had positive exchanges. When I really stood back and looked at things objectively, I could see that most of the time I was what I think of as a 'good' mom. I show up for my son in loving ways, and I'm usually calm, supportive, and caring. We have a great relationship. I cut myself some slack, I guess. And when I stopped labeling myself as a bad mom, I noticed I was more able to keep my cool when things got chaotic or when he was having a meltdown. Instead of losing it, I stayed calm and we worked together to get through it."

I nodded and added, "So you had been overgeneralizing by letting some occasional yelling incidents dictate your opinion of yourself as a mom, and to get past it, you used objective thinking to create a more accurate assessment of how you're doing as a mom. Does that sound right?"

She smiled and said, "Yep! That's what worked for me. I know

I'm doing the best I can, and it helps me to remain as objective as possible. It's hard, I'll say that, but it's helpful."

Kelly discovered for herself how to break a pattern of overgeneralizing, and that is with objective thinking. And it got her back into her authenticity; it helped her see that her Best Self would never label herself as a bad mom. When we are looking at something objectively, that means we are looking at the situation as a whole instead of compartmentalizing and hyper-focusing on specific moments in time or specific events in the past. When you consider *all* parts of a whole, you are able to judge it with far more accuracy.

THE OVERGENERALIZING BELIEF CYCLE

Because I want you to know just how quickly you can make changes by tapping into the positive FORCE, I'm going to share a coaching session I did with a colleague, Eva. When she arrived at my house, I was taken aback by her appearance. She had such sadness in her eyes. There was a heaviness about her, as if she'd been weighted down and was just dragging herself along as best she could. I've known Eva for years, so I knew this wasn't how she usually appeared, but this was the first time we'd ever sat down to discuss anything going on in her life. Here's how that conversation went.

"As I think you know, one of the most important things in my life has always been helping others. I'm a co-founder of a psychiatric supportive living home, and it's been my primary focus."

I know Eva to be such a hard worker, and everyone in the recovery community knows she has such a huge heart. Nodding emphatically, I replied, "Yes, you've really done amazing things there. And I know you have several kids too, right?"

Beaming at the thought of her kids, she said, "I'm a single mother of adult children. I have a thirty-one-year-old son, a thirty-year-old son, a twenty-seven-year-old daughter, and a twelve-year-old son."

"Got it. Four kids! And you're sober—how long?"

"I'm nineteen years sober. I was addicted to methamphetamine, alcohol, and I smoked marijuana—really, anything that just sent me into oblivion."

"Okay. And your kids, I think you've mentioned that they have different dads?"

Immediately casting her eyes down to her lap, she paused for just a moment, seeming to gather her strength, and then continued, "Yes, absolutely. It's all part of my story. All four of my kids have different dads. When I was born, my mom had tuberculosis and I contracted it, so I was immediately put in a baby hospital for the first full year of my life. That's how they handled it back then; they'd only recently discovered the cure, and it meant many months in the hospital. I didn't realize it until I was thirty years old, but because I was removed from my mother upon birth, I never attached. I started out life in a sterile hospital setting, and not nearly enough human interaction. I developed what they call an attachment disorder."

I could tell she'd told this story before, but it's a significant piece of her past, and it took strength to retell it. She carried on, "Later, as an adult, I chose relationships that were void of any kind of intimacy. In fact, one of those men was schizophrenic. Another was extremely violent and actually got deported because he almost killed me. And one"—she slowed down, took a breath, and continued—"one turned out to be running one of the largest child pornography rings in the U.S. And I had trusted him with my kids day in and day out. One of my biggest regrets of my life. I later learned he sexually violated one of my sons. He was arrested and he is now in prison. It was so terrible when it all happened. It was all over the news and everything. Awful."

Shifting the conversation slightly, I asked, "You must have been pretty young when you started having your children. How old were you?"

"I was twenty when I had my first one, twenty-one when I had my second one."

"And were you sober then?" I asked.

"The way I describe it I wasn't *awake*. You know? I wasn't like completely a drug addict; I was more addicted to having relationships and finding someone to love me and take care of me. I'm from a Mexican family, and I just always thought that's what you do."

"What about the father of your twelve-year-old?" I asked.

She said, "I met him in my sobriety. But I got into a relationship and I hadn't worked on any of those things yet, only on the drug addiction. I married him anyway. He was a sober sex addict until he wasn't sober anymore. It was the whole illusion. We had a house, we had everything. I got pregnant, and next thing you know, I'm learning about all of his affairs, his extracurricular sexual relationships. I got out of that relationship and I went into treatment. Thank God. I got to meet people who actually helped me. I did lots of therapy and inner-child work, and I made peace with my past, especially my trauma from birth. It finally all made sense—all the decisions I'd made." Just talking about the work she's done in therapy seemed to give her more energy. She seemed less agitated and as if she were breathing more deeply.

"Thank you for sharing all of this with me. If you think about your 'billboard problem' in your life, what is that for you?" I asked.

She said, "The billboard problem is this: I'm going to be alone, I'm going to be poor, and I'm going to have regrets about not having all the things I dreamed of."

"And how long have you had these thoughts?" I asked.

"It comes and goes, but probably my whole life," she admitted.

"Do you remember having these thoughts as a little girl?"

"Yeah, I would get scared sometimes and I'd see my dad, wasted drunk, and I would feel so scared and unsafe like I was going to be alone. Do you know what I mean?"

"Yes. I would call it your Boogeyman, that thing we carry into our adult life that's not real but we've been trained to believe is real. The thing under the bed seems real, and we look for signs that it is; certain events can trigger us. And your Boogeyman is that you're going to be alone and poor and have regrets."

Tears welling in her eyes, she quietly said, "Yeah."

"So, here's what I think we should do. There's something I refer to as the FORCE, and it's what drives our decision making. The FORCE represents specific ways we tend to perceive situations, patterns we fall into for one reason or another. One of those is overgeneralizing, and that's what I think you've been doing."

Eva nodded, and started to shift a bit in her seat.

"Can you already see where we're going?" I asked, smiling.

"Yes, I think so," she said.

"Okay, let's talk about your belief, or your fear, that you're going to end up alone. Where do you think that comes from?"

Almost eager to answer this question, she replied, "I've had four relationships that were absolute disasters. I'm lucky to have survived them, frankly," she said.

"So, if we think about the idea of overgeneralizing, which is when we judge ourselves based on specific incidents, do you think that's what you're doing in terms of your relationships?"

"Well, I know I'm really scared to be in a relationship now."

"But are you open to being in one?"

"Sometimes yes, and sometimes no. I can't pick men. I have a broken picker," she said.

"Are you open to the idea that you could have a better picker?"

"Yes," she said.

"Was the guy you chose when you were sober better than your previous choices?"

"Yes, a little bit."

"But when you think about dating, do you think things like 'Oh, it's going to be a disaster because it has been in the past'?" I asked.

"Oh yeah, I'll say things like that. Someone says to me I should get on a dating app and I say, 'My luck is I would get a serial killer.'" She laughed, but it was clear she wasn't really joking.

"When you're looking at it as an obstacle of being alone, and you overgeneralize saying all the guys you pick are bad, there's not much gray in there; your thinking is pretty black and white. Would you say that's true?"

"Yes," she said as she fought back tears.

"Okay, so now let's try viewing this as an opportunity. So, the facts are what, if you're viewing it as an opportunity?"

"I have been in relationships in the past, I have done recovery work, I've spent a lot of time alone with myself, being in relationship with myself, I've opened up a business, I've been a part of a successful business. But then I get to *that* part," she says, and laughs out loud.

"The alone part?" I asked. She nodded. I asked, "How can you be open to the idea of you *not* being alone?"

Thinking, she replied, "I can go on a date?"

"Yeah, you could go on a date. You could think about it differently," I said.

Without a moment's pause she said, "But then what if I never find the right person?"

I said, "I'm single. One could look at my life and go, 'Why is he single? Why hasn't he had someone with him for the past ten years? Or why hasn't he settled down?' One could say that, but I have enough faith in the universe that even our bad experiences make us stronger, better. We don't actually have control. We can't control other people wanting us and we can't control us wanting other people." I paused and then said, "And I think it's about the story that you're telling yourself: that you are somehow a failure, you have a bad picker, and you're scared because you're not believing that your judgment knows what's best for you. Does that feel right?"

Now starting to sob, Eva said, "Yeah, it does."

"So, it's a story, regardless of the relationship, that's just part of what has gotten you into this way of thinking of relationships as obstacles and bad, and that you're somehow not good enough and you can't figure it out. And you're afraid you're going to be alone, but . . . you're alone right now and you're doing just fine. Right?"

"Yeah, but I stay busy so I don't think about it," she said, now laughing.

"Earlier you mentioned a dream. What is your dream? I mean, I look at you, and you have four kids who are artistic, healthy, creative," I said.

"I love being with my kids, they're so talented. I love watching their shows. To see them being successful and to know that we made it out of all that. Not a lot of people would make it out of what we went through," she said.

"And that's who you are, someone who made it through, learned, got wiser. What's this regret thing you mentioned then?"

"I guess regrets about myself, you know? Regrets if I'm alone, if I look into my future and see myself alone. I don't want to be that old lady living by herself in an apartment. It's a scary-ass thought. That's what I mean."

"But you've been capable throughout this. With four different dads, super-complex situations, you still have gotten to the other side, and you have a business that's doing well, so we know you are capable of doing things on your own," I said.

"I guess I just don't know if I am capable of finding a great relationship," she said.

"But when you say that, you're overgeneralizing again. You're telling yourself that because you've been in bad relationships in the past, you will always be in bad relationships. What if you didn't overgeneralize by telling yourself that story about being a bad picker, and instead you used objective thinking? Then you could take the focus off your fear of repeating a pattern and see that you *are* capable of choosing the right person, or that you are actually at peace being on your own. Then you could be more open to all possibilities and opportunities. Have you chosen people who aren't healthy for you in the past? Yeah, we all have! But that does not mean you always will in the future. And culture has this belief about needing to get married, to find our 'one and only.' But the truth is, that's not realistic for everyone, and that's okay."

The statistics back me up on that point too, as they continue to show that marriage is no guarantee of lasting love; the divorce rate continues to hover around 50 percent.

She said, "That makes sense, for sure. And I want to tell myself a different story, I really do. I've worked so hard to change all of that negativity inside of me—through therapy and everything. But sometimes I get frustrated that it's still here, inside me."

I asked, "Your beliefs about yourself?"

"Yeah, I know there's blockage because of it. That fear is just— there. I don't want to be fearful anymore. I know there's importance to me, that I matter, and that I'm worthy. I think I just forget."

"What's a decision you can make today so that you don't forget that you're deserving and that you're capable?"

She thought about that for a moment and then said, "I think I need to reconnect with my true friends, people I trust and who believe in me."

"That sounds like a great decision. So your first step is to increase your social life so you create a community who reminds you of how great you are. How can you do that?"

"It's about scheduling it in, making time for it," she said, with determination in her voice.

"So how can you be empowered when you leave here today? Shifting out of 'I'm going to be alone, poor, and with regrets' requires what action?"

"I'm going to spend more time being social. I have a couple of friends I can call today," she said.

"Cool. So, you're making a commitment to your social life, and then in terms of dating or relationships, does it feel better to make no decisions at this point?"

"Yeah, no decisions on relationships right now. I want to strengthen my social life, focus on self-care, and then I will be in a better place to think about a relationship," she said.

"Cool. So, do you feel set on your next steps?"

"Yes! I really do," she said, with a new air of confidence.

When we finished talking, Eva's eyes were brighter, and she literally seemed lighter in her seat. She had experienced a breakthrough that came from shifting her perspective. Eva went from feeling defeated, deflated, and dark because all she saw was obstacles, to feeling enlightened, empowered, and elated when she started to see opportunities. Specifically, she started to see in what ways she had been overgeneralizing about her intimate relationships. That awareness then allowed her to choose objective thinking instead, and understand that her past does not have to dictate her future. Her fears about being alone could no longer keep her stuck in that obstacle mindset.

Eva did "rally the troops" and immediately set about surrounding herself with friends who would help her remain objective. She assembled a team that motivated her, inspired her, and most important helped her make decisions as her Best Self. And you know what? The last time we spoke, she said the last thing on her mind was finding a relationship. "So what if I end up as that old lady alone in my apartment? I'll just call some friends to come over!" She'd gone from overgeneralizing by believing she had a "broken picker," and would surely end up alone as a result, to looking at it objectively, realizing that she was perfectly capable of choosing a healthy relationship, but that in fact she didn't want or need one right now anyway!

I want to say it again: this kind of transformation does not require years in therapy. It's truly about shifting your perspective, and it can absolutely be accomplished by identifying One Decision you can make toward a better life.

THE POSITIVE FORCE: OBJECTIVE THINKING

Take a look at this comparison of these two *Os* in the FORCE acronym, and notice the stark differences in the two perspectives.

We are thinking objectively when we have our eyes wide open, and we are looking at all aspects of the person or situation, rather than allowing a preconceived notion to guide our opinion. Critical thinking is essentially a synonym for objective thinking: it's removing our ignorance.

Objective thinking allows us to be curious, to put our own assumptions aside. Objective thinking frees us up to have new ideas and to adopt new belief systems. When we are thinking objectively, rather than having the tunnel vision that overgeneralizing brings about, we are more able to evolve in our lives. Progressiveness comes from objective thinking. And I also believe it allows us to be empathetic and compassionate, toward us and toward others. Because of that, there's more peace—both inner and outer peace—when we are thinking objectively.

Overgeneralizing:	Objective Thinking:
• Drawing conclusions based on one stand-alone incident. • Labeling entire groups of people based on one person or experience. • Labeling ourselves as a result of one event.	• Considering all aspects of yourself, someone else, or a situation, not just an isolated moment in time. • Being curious and flexible. • Exploring new beliefs, embracing new ideas, and adopting new ways of thinking. • Exhibiting empathy and compassion; better able to appreciate someone else's point of view.

OVERGENERALIZING IN SOCIETY

Though this chapter focuses on ways in which overgeneralizing can derail you from your attempts at reinventing, evolving, or pivoting to create a better life, I do want to give you a brief example of how this way of thinking can play out in society at large. I think we should all be keenly aware of this so that we can stop ourselves from doing it.

I often take my labradoodle, Vida Maria, on walks. If you are a pet owner, then you know how much our animals mean to us, and we want to take great care of them. When she and I are out walking at night, we encounter quite a few individuals who are homeless. Some of them unfortunately appear to be suffering from mental illness, some have told me that they were kicked out of their houses, some are on drugs, and others are not. Their backstories run the gamut; none of these individuals' stories are exactly alike.

A lot of the homeless folks I talk to while on my walks are kind. They ask how I'm doing, they pet Vida, and they say things like "God bless you" and "Thank you for talking to me and not pretending like I'm not here." I have met one person, however, who is not kind to me. He's tried to spit on me before and often calls me, and others, rude names. I'll refer to him as Dave. I've heard from various neighbors that they've also had "interesting" experiences with Dave. In fact, the owner of the local barbershop even told me that Dave recently stood in his front window, dropped his pants, and flashed everyone getting a haircut. Now, again, Dave's behavior is not at all indicative of that of the overall homeless population in my area, or in society. But he draws a lot of attention to himself with the choices he makes.

I was curious to learn about how my neighbors view the homeless population, so I asked several folks for their opinions in a little informal poll I conducted. Mostly, folks weren't overly concerned about it, or they had compassionate responses and wished there was something they could do to help. But one person immediately scowled when I asked the question and said venomously, "Did you hear about what that one homeless dude did the other day? He was flashing people. Disgusting. The homeless are just awful. They are a blight on the neighborhood, driving down our home values and committing crimes. The cops should be rounding them all up."

He's entitled to his opinion, but I share this because it's a prime example of an overgeneralization. Was Dave's behavior inappropriate and illegal? Yes. But is it logical or fair to point to one homeless man's behavior and suggest that it is symbolic of an entire population of people? Absolutely not. Overgeneralizing about people is dangerous and unethical. We must be vigilant in our self-awareness and make sure we're not judging groups of people based on one experience or one person. I'm sure you can see how racism, sexism, and all the isms have their roots in overgeneralizing, and why we want to be so cautious about it.

HOW OUR BRAINS CAN TRICK US INTO OVERGENERALIZING

Sometimes our tendency to overgeneralize can feel like a knee-jerk reaction. We aren't purposely doing it; it's just second nature. That is because of shortcuts that our brains create. As you know, not every problem we encounter in life allows us the time to thoughtfully calculate our decisions. There are many times when we need to make a snap judgment and run with it. This is why our brains are wired to reduce that complexity by creating shortcuts.

One such shortcut has to do with representation; it's when we are ignoring statistics and focusing instead on mental examples, or stereotypes. We might compare a present situation with the most representative mental example we can think of. Here's an example: Let's say you are trying to decide if someone is trustworthy. You might compare aspects of the person with other mental examples you hold. Maybe an elderly woman reminds you of your grandmother in appearance (she's about the same age, wears similar clothes, or has the same hairstyle), so you automatically assume that she is similar to your grandmother in other ways—that she is kind, gentle, and trustworthy.

Another common shortcut we use when making decisions is based on how easily we can bring something to mind. When faced with a decision, we might call upon relevant examples we've seen or experienced. Based on which examples we can quickly recall, we might believe those to be more common or frequently occurring. Here's an example: If you are planning a trip and deciding whether to fly there, and suddenly think of a number of recent airline accidents, you might conclude that air travel is too risky and opt to drive instead. But in actuality, plane crashes are less common than car crashes, so the availability shortcut has actually skewed your decision making in this case.

Here's the intrinsic problem with these shortcuts: we often blindly trust them, and we can even confuse them with a gut feeling, but they *can* be incorrect. We want to be aware when we are using these mental shortcuts so that we can purposely test them for validity before overly relying on them.

OVERGENERALIZING OR OBJECTIVE THINKING?

Take a look at this chart to get an idea of how we tend to overgeneralize, as opposed to ways we could think objectively. Think about how overgeneralizing can lead to decisions that are not authentic to who we really are, and how the objective thinking examples could lead us to make decisions that feel better to us.

OVERGENERALIZING	OBJECTIVE THINKING
All diets don't work.	A lot of people have had success on diets.
People aren't trustworthy.	I'm trustworthy, so I know others must be!
Guys just want younger women.	A lot of men are faithful, even as the relationship matures.
I've always been depressed.	It's impossible to be depressed 100 percent of the time, because then you wouldn't even know what depression looks like, as you'd have nothing to compare it with.

EXERCISE

What's a problem in your life today?

_____

_____

_____

_____

_____

How could you be overgeneralizing in that problem area?

_____

_____

_____

_____

_____

Now, what are some ways you could approach those areas by thinking objectively instead?

_____

_____

_____

_____

_____

_____

What are the opportunities revealed by thinking objectively instead of overgeneralizing? List them here.

_____

_____

_____

_____

_____

_____

What's a decision you could make based upon that opportunity-minded objective thinking?

_____

_____

_____

_____

_____

_____

Are you ready to take some form of action? Or are you at peace with things as they are? Write your answer here:

_____

_____

_____

_____

_____

_____

Now that you've made a decision, can you let go of the outcome?

OBJECTIVELY MOVING FORWARD

As we head into the next letter in the acronym, keep your objective-thinking cap on, because we'll be looking at an unexpected FORCE that is so deeply rooted it can create arguments, resentments, and even wars—between countries, between friends, and even within yourself.

7

FORCE

RIGID MINDSET OR RELAXED MINDSET

The *R* of FORCE stands for a rigid mindset or a relaxed mindset. One is more set in its ways, and the other is flexible to the changing events, people, places, or things in life. Think of a strong, old oak tree that's been around for more than one hundred years, until a huge storm with gale-force winds comes blowing into town, and—wham!—that strong, unbending tree is suddenly uprooted. Now think about palm trees and how they react in hurricanes, for instance. You've probably seen news coverage of a hurricane or tropical storm making landfall, and the palm trees are all bent horizontal, blowing this way and that in the wind. But when the storm is over, they go right back to standing tall and proud. Why? Their trunks are extremely flexible, or relaxed, if you will. They have a lot of give when the wind is blowing. They can go with the flow, and that's what keeps them alive.

The same is true in our decisions. When our mindset is rigid, we are easily "uprooted" by the stress and unexpected turbulence, and we aren't able to make decisions as our Best Self when we're being so dogmatic. On the flip side, when we're relaxed, we are better at adapting, and allowing the winds of life to blow around us, without jeopardizing our authenticity.

When we are being rigid, we are believing we can control outcomes or that we can control other people and their decisions. Here are some examples of how rigidity plays out in our lives:

- Having a "my way or the highway" mentality.

- Right fighting—a need to be right in every exchange/have the last word.

- "Should" statements—when we or someone else says we "should" or "should not" do something, according to our strict belief system.

- Believing that the way you've always done things is the only way to do them.

This can show up in a number of ways, and it can be tough to identify in ourselves, though pretty easy to spot in others. We all know someone we might classify as rigid—that person who wants things done a specific way, and there's no convincing them that another way might work. I'll give you an example from my own life.

I shared with you earlier that I worked for a company long ago that specialized in helping families intervene on loved ones struggling with addiction so that they could get the treatment or help they needed. The interventions I did were primarily with people struggling with major mental health or addictive disorders, and either their families, employers, or friends hired me to help. Interventions are last-ditch efforts. The reasons someone hires an interventionist are usually a medical crisis, a judge's ruling, or some other major outside force to get someone to make a decision to get well. It is often hard for people struggling with addiction to change unless the people, places, and things around them also change.

This is why people bring in an interventionist. They all could just arrange a sit-down meeting with the person they are concerned about, and trust me, a lot of families have tried that and it hasn't worked, so they ended up hiring me. They needed structure and a plan of action that created the best possible outcome. The company I first started doing interventions with more than fifteen years ago primarily did the Johnson model of intervention. A foundational element of this model is to surprise the person. We would have a family member wake up to see his entire family, some colleagues, family friends, mentors, and so forth sitting in the living room while they squinted and rubbed their eyes, typically in their pajamas. The company I worked for utilized the Johnson model of intervention because it works. This type of intervention helps loved ones to stop enabling, and it helps get someone into treatment.

There are three letters that the family members write. The first letter begins, "I've seen your addiction affect your life in the following ways." In this letter a person may outline the characteristics of how the person has changed. An example of a line from this letter is "I have seen an upbeat, loving, positive person turn into an angry, mean, selfish friend who doesn't care about me." Another one might be "I have seen a person who had passion, drive, and a lot of success turn into someone who has been jobless for several years," or "I have seen a parent who loved their kids and showed up at school events turn into someone who ignores their kids and puts drinking alcohol ahead of them." The purpose of this letter is to tell the person being intervened on exactly why everyone is concerned. Believe it or not, it's very common for the person being intervened on to believe everyone is overreacting or that it's some kind of conspiracy, despite ample evidence to the contrary, such as having been arrested for driving under the influence, kids crying and telling them about their drinking problem, or getting fired from their job.

The second letter, which is read after the first one, begins, "Your addiction has affected my life in the following ways." The person reading this letter typically shows one of three emotions: sadness/crying, numbness/lack of emotion, or anger. Examples of statements they might read are "I have had to lie to our friends and family by telling them you are okay. I am so stressed and anxious about your crises that I'm no longer effective in my job. I lose sleep and worry constantly that you are going to kill yourself and somehow it will be my fault."

The last letter begins, "If you decide not to accept the help that is being offered here today, you need to know that our relationship will change in the following ways." When that happens, you can imagine the person you're intervening on has a very strong reaction. Usually there's anger in some form. It's obvious that the person needs help, but you cannot force adults to get help. Ultimately it is their decision.

Over 90 percent of the time, I had people in treatment within a few days of an intervention by sticking to the script and process. There were the rare times that, although I stuck to this script and process, people didn't choose to go. But I can tell you when this did happen, it was usually because a family member was not willing to stop enabling the person. It would be because a parent was telling his son or daughter that they would have to move out, but then did not follow through. Interestingly, I have found that for some in interventions keeping themselves from enabling their family member or friend is just as hard as it is for the person choosing to get help. It was really important, then, that I help the family stick to their bottom lines so the whole system could get well.

There was a script the organization had created for interventions, and all of the counselors had to follow that script, *no matter what*. The script was solid, and nine times out of ten it was appropriate. But as you might imagine, when you're doing an intervention with a family, there are many variables. These things pretty much never play out "as expected." That's because when someone is deep into an addiction, their behaviors are unpredictable, often erratic. I have had people pull out guns on me, I once had a woman jump out of a window to escape intervention and break her leg, I have walked in on folks having affairs because of the unexpected nature of the intervention, and I have intervened on people who had written a suicide note and were planning to take their own lives in the next twenty-four hours. I had to be able to adapt to any situation; that was a necessary part of the job. However, the company was so rigid in the way they wanted their interventions to play out, that it left very little room for adaptability. I understood the need for this with my first twenty to thirty interventions, but at a certain point I had become an expert and my intuition along with experience was what made me great.

One of the rules set forth by the company was that you never leave the family. Well, I'll never forget one intervention in particular, when the alcoholic took off to another part of the house. The rules said I should stay with the family, but my intuition said to follow him and talk to him. I broke the company's rule, and I talked to him one-on-one. Here's what happened.

Bill's family and wife had hired me and brought me in. When I got there, he was asleep. When he came out of the bedroom and everyone read their letters to him, he said he loved them very much but he was not going to treatment. He specifically said he was not going because of the way they chose to intervene on him. I'd seen people go from crying to anger really fast in an intervention. When he got to the anger, he took off to the bedroom. My gut told me he needed someone who was not family to talk to him. I went in, sat on his bed, and said, "Look, I know this sucks. No one wants this to happen to them. It's embarrassing. Clearly everyone here loves you. But, man, are you really going to risk losing your relationships? You can go to rehab! Help me understand what's coming up for you. You really want your wife to divorce you, and to have issues with your kids? Why would you make your life harder? You're being so adamant that this was not the right way to intervene on you, but can you look beyond that?" We talked it out, and fifteen minutes later I walked out and said, "He's good to go. I'm flying with him to treatment." And he is still sober to this day.

Later that week, on a conference call with supervisors, they expressed that how I'd handled the situation was inappropriate because it went against their policy. But at the end of the day, I accomplished the overall goal: he was in rehab. Now, of course there is a need for uniformity or standard operating procedures in this case and many others. But when someone is in the field, as I was, especially for a potentially life-threatening situation, and that person has been trained to handle such situations, there should be enough flexibility built in to allow employees to handle whatever might arise. I believed at the time, as I do to this day, that Bill would not have gone to rehab had I not handled the intervention in the way that I did, so I'm glad I took a relaxed approach and adapted to the situation. I was able to connect with my Best Self and make the decision from that place, rather than from dogma.

This is just one example of how a rigid stance can stand in the way of progress and potentially prevent the best possible outcome. I'm not suggesting you "go rogue" at work, necessarily. In my case, it was a matter of life or death, and I needed to rely on my intuition. In those situations, you sometimes have to make decisions that you believe will save someone's life. It's very different from making a decision simply because we don't agree with a policy.

HOW RIGIDITY SHOWS UP

Now, you might be wondering how rigidity can affect our decision making. Well, it can mean that while trying to land on a wise decision, we get so caught up in the details of a problem or in the specific methods we would typically use for solving it that we miss the big picture. We miss the opportunities for success, for trying new methods or calling on new knowledge, research, or understanding. Particularly when we are looking to pivot in any area of life, or to create change, we *must* be willing to try something new.

Another way to envision the tangible results of a rigid mindset is to think about that parent who has strict, no-nonsense household rules and who has very little desire or ability to adjust them. If a child walks in the door from being out in the rain and is soaking wet, that parent might say, "You are filthy and wet! Leave those shoes outside where they belong and do not drip on the clean floor!" Whereas a more relaxed parent might react by saying, "Wow, looks like you had fun! Would you mind cleaning off those muddy shoes before you come in?"

You can see, hear, and feel the difference, right? The FORCE of energy we put toward others is going to determine how we feel and how they feel, especially when we're talking to a child. It can be exhausting spending time with people who tend to be rigid in their thinking. They can be so dogmatic in their viewpoints that you just feel like you're invisible, or that you're always "wrong" in their opinion. It can feel defeating if someone is always correcting you, or explaining why "their way" is better. You might feel like you can't win, and that's not motivating in the least. I purposely do not surround myself with a lot of rigid individuals, especially if I've seen them go to unnecessary lengths to be rigid in some way. When people are obviously trying to get control, it doesn't feel good.

When we adopt a rigid state of mind in general, or about specific areas or topics of life, we are ensconced in a set of rules and we refuse to consider that a better way might exist. It's "my way or the highway" when we are being rigid. This mentality is very common in people who are right fighters, meaning they are more focused on being right than on the actual content of the argument or discussion. Sometimes we become rigid in our thinking because we believe this is the way we've always done things, so it must be the right way. Rigidity often means being so caught up in what we believe is right that we miss what is in our best interest.

If we are rigid in our thinking, we tend to play small. The very notion of creating a better life, a bigger life, a life that is more deeply fulfilling to us, can feel overwhelming because it would require making changes to a set of rules by which we live. The idea of it might cause anxiety. When we are being rigid, it's likely because it feels safe. It's worked before, it'll work again, don't deviate—that's how you might look at life. But at some point, just because it worked before doesn't mean it works now, because life evolves and we need to evolve with it.

In many cases, I've found that folks who exercise rigidity do so because of a family legacy. They grew up in a rigid environment and continued that theme in their adult life. Or they saw everyone in the family acting the same way or making similar choices, so it just felt right to follow suit. It can be hard to break out of those long-term patterns or to adapt in any way.

I've fallen into the trap myself. When I started the podcast *Always Evolving with Coach Mike Bayer*, I had this very specific vision for how each episode would play out. I wanted to record them all at my house, and I wanted to create a certain vibe. I believed each episode needed to be perfect. I was being so precious about every single detail, to the point that it became a perfectionist approach. I had a specific vision for the media rollout to promote the podcast, so when we spelled a guest's name incorrectly in a newspaper article, I was completely thrown off kilter. My need for perfection was crushed. I wanted to videotape all of them for YouTube, and that didn't work out either. I was forced to let go of my rigid ideas about the podcast and relax. As it turned out, we recorded my first interview, which was with Jessica Simpson right as her book was coming out, in a tiny little dressing room at a venue where she'd been speaking. If I had not relaxed my vision, I would've missed the chance to do that great interview. I realized that at the end of the day all those details that I wanted to be "just so" were actually *so* insignificant.

The surprises on the podcast journey just kept coming. My second episode was with Dr. Phil, and it took place at his house. We had a fascinating discussion, and he revealed more details about his life in that conversation than he ever had in an interview. Producers who had been working with him for more than twenty years even commented that they learned new information about Dr. Phil in my podcast interview. My third episode was with Vivica A. Fox, and that one took place in a converted edit bay on a movie lot. You just never know how things are going to play out! My willingness to let go of my rigid ideas and relax into the flow of how life and the universe were delivering me interviews for my new podcast is what has catapulted me toward success. I took myself out of the box I'd created, and then a world of opportunity became visible. Success is not a destination; it is a journey, and if we're too rigid, we miss the journey.

THE DEAF EARS DECISION

A prime example of rigidity is when someone will go to any length to not hear another point of view on any given topic. In fact, there was a study that showed that members of a specific political party are so averse to hearing the other side that two-thirds of study participants gave up the chance to win money just to avoid having to listen to the other side. People siloed topics such as same-sex marriage, elections, marijuana, climate change, guns, and abortion into "right" or "wrong." They so strongly believed their perspective was correct that they had no interest in hearing evidence to the contrary.

We all know someone like this. They're so convinced their stance is right that they shut down any and all information you might throw at them that isn't in alignment with their beliefs. There are a lot of problems with this mindset, but the most obvious one is that it makes success nearly

(continued)

impossible. A big factor in being successful is being relaxed, flexible, and capable of hearing and absorbing the opinions and ideas of others. People prefer working with others who are relaxed, versus rigid. Rigidity can easily lead to conflict, whereas a relaxed state of mind can lead to collaboration and resolution. Keep this at the top of your mind as you think about areas of your life where you might be rigid, but you would benefit from relaxing and opening your ears a bit to others' thoughts.

RECOGNIZING RIGIDITY IN OUR DECISION MAKING

Let's spend some time understanding in which areas of life you might have a rigid mindset and how that might be affecting your ability to make decisions as your Best Self. A rigid mindset means you're viewing life, and everything it might throw at you, as an obstacle. Think about what area is currently creating the most tension for you. I like to start there because rigidity comes from tension, from the need for control, or from trying to keep everything in a box. It's helpful to recognize that so much of what we're being rigid about right now simply will not matter a year from now.

Okay, now that you're focused on a particularly tense or stress-ful aspect of your life, think about something specific that might set you off within it. For instance, if your job feels stressful, is there a particular co-worker who has a negative effect on you? Maybe he tends to be lazy, to take credit for others' work, or to show up late for meetings. Does this spark something in you that makes you want to toss him the office handbook and remind him of the "way you do things around there"? Or perhaps you have a child, and when she misbehaves or acts in a way that you interpret as disrespectful, you get upset and remind her that "as long as she lives under your roof, she is to follow your rules."

Being rigid can present in very subtle ways. We often focus on extreme examples of it, but it doesn't always manifest itself as that extreme. For example, if you're getting back on the dating scene following a breakup or divorce, do you find yourself annoyed by people you meet who hold different opinions from you, whether it's in politics, in religion, or maybe even in the college football team they root for? Does it just tick you off to no end that an oth-erwise "quality" person could possibly hold this "incorrect" view? Do you try to convince them of the "right" viewpoint, or maybe just vow never to go out with them again?

A lot of clients I've worked with struggle with businesses they've started, and even though their business is not especially lucrative, or does not bring them much joy, they hang on in the belief that they have to keep it going. They refuse to make that difficult decision to let it go. They feel like they've already invested all this time, energy, money, blood, sweat, and tears, and they can't possibly shut the business down and do something different. In their mind, there's no going back. But if they relax, and see the value in the experience and wisdom they gained, it's much easier to see that it might be time for a change.

Here are some more questions to get you thinking:

- Do you ever find yourself arguing more than you'd like to?

- Do you approach problems with aggression? Do you get aggressive toward others?

- Do you look for validation from others to confirm your own beliefs?

Do the behaviors or opinions of others trigger you to be rigid, firmer in your own beliefs/truths, and completely unbending as opposed to relaxed, willing to meet them where they are, and even open to the possibility of adjusting your own opinions? Do you make decisions simply to justify your previous actions or beliefs, as if to "prove" yourself right?

Think about these questions as we continue through the chapter, and at the end you will be doing an exercise to help you further uncover ways in which you might be rigid in your life and decision making.

THE POSITIVE FORCE: RELAXED MINDSET

A relaxed mindset means you're viewing life, and everything it might throw at you, as an opportunity. Being relaxed can help you overcome a rigid mindset when looking at a problem. I define relaxed in this context as being centered. When we are approaching life from a relaxed mindset, we are more likely to accept life on life's terms instead of always trying to dictate it. We take the time to make others feel seen and heard, and we are willing to try new ideas and concepts. Unafraid to pivot in a new direction or maybe even make the occasional reinvention U-turn, being relaxed means being flexible and open. In this state of mind, we might ask, "Is it going to matter five years from now?" That perspective helps alleviate some of the pressure of certain decisions.

When we are in a relaxed mindset, we are not reactive, and instead we are centered. By being willing to let go of the rigidity and do things differently, you will very likely discover new opportunities. When you're relaxed in your life, you're not trying to control, and you're more able to receive opportunities.

Another amazing side effect of a relaxed mindset is that it allows us to see our lives in a new, fresh light. We trust ourselves to make changes because we aren't obsessed with the outcome, or with being right all the time. We place a higher value on progress than we do on being correct. Anytime you find yourself feeling tense as you try to decide on your next move, it's imperative to find a way to relax within it. You see, even though the answer may not be apparent to you right now, and even if others aren't acting or reacting in the way you wish they would, you can still decide to have peace in the moment.

Each of us has our own unique methods for finding our way toward a relaxed point of view. For me, if I put on a Bob Marley song, I can almost instantly feel more relaxed. And I'm not just referring to a bodily sense of relaxation, like I'm ready to take a snooze by the pool. Yes, the physical relaxation is part of it, but it's also a mental relaxation. It's about releasing our ego and getting outside ourselves. Rigidity comes from a belief that we know best. But the reality is, we *don't* always know best. Sometimes we need the wisdom and experience of someone else to guide us. And sometimes we need life to teach us something new.

So, what can you do that will help you to release those parts of yourself that are holding on so tightly to your belief systems and open you up to new possibilities? Is it meditation? Is it a yoga class? Are there specific mantras you could try out to help you get into that state of mind? Perhaps if you connect with your spirituality through prayer, you could reconnect with your Best Self and allow any rigidity to dissipate? Or are there people in your life you can talk to who have made very different decisions in life from you, people you could learn from? Is there a friend or family member whose relaxed approach has helped them make a positive change, or even feel more at peace with an outcome? There are many ways to open yourself up to receiving new ideas and opportunities.

In thinking about the area(s) you are looking to improve in your life right now, consider whether you could encourage a more open,

flexible, and relaxed perspective that might help you either see a
new opportunity or just feel less stressed out and anxious about it.
Write your thoughts here:

_____

_____

_____

_____

_____

THERE'S SUCH A THING AS *TOO* RELAXED!

In the spectrum between rigid and relaxed, it's important we don't go too far in one direction or another. We've talked about the ways in which being too rigid can negatively impact us, but it can be equally detrimental if we slide too far down the scale toward overly relaxed. I mean, no one wants to get in a plane with a pilot who is relaxed to the point of unfocused, right? And it's never great to work with people who are late to every single meeting. And if we're too relaxed about paying parking tickets, we will eventually pay the price in

(continued)

the form of a boot on our tire. And parents who set no rules or boundaries at all for their children will end up in a chaotic household run by screaming kids. What I'm saying is that we need to temper our relaxation with a healthy dose of another *R* word: responsibility.

As you make decisions in your life, you want to look at them through a relaxed lens, one that allows you to consider all angles, but without forgoing responsibility. There is a big difference between relaxed and irresponsible. You have to be accountable for your part in it, and make sure your decision does not endanger yourself or someone else. You, and only you, are responsible for the decisions you make.

IT'S NOT THAT SERIOUS

Part of a relaxed mindset means being able to laugh at ourselves, which is a key ingredient to staying authentic. In fact, a good litmus test for whether you're taking a rigid or relaxed approach to your decision making is to see if you can make a little fun of yourself in the process. I'll give you an example from my own life.

Shortly after *Best Self* came out, I launched a Best Self Challenge online, where folks would draw their Best Self and Anti-Self and share them to inspire others. I had a very specific vision in mind for a fun video I'd use to announce the challenge online. This was during the final season of *Game of Thrones*, which was getting a huge amount of buzz. I'd been watching that show from the beginning myself, and I was a big fan. So I had this idea to become a White Walker and then share my Best Self and Anti-Self as the White Walker. Oh yeah, I'm serious.

I went all out with this plan—I mean, full-on showbiz. I bought an intricate costume to fit my six-foot-five frame, I paid for a professional movie makeup artist, I even ordered bright blue contact lenses so I could truly transform into a White Walker from head to toe. As I was struggling to get this thick blue contact in my eye, my assistant trying desperately to help, my eyes started tearing up and causing the makeup to run all down my face, so the makeup artist was trying to get in there and do damage control . . . it was a whole thing. I was a hot mess. (And those stupid contacts made my eyes hurt for days afterward!)

My version of a *Game of Thrones* White Walker, moments before he sat down with Coach Mike to discuss his Best Self (Sugar Walker) and Anti-Self (Luke Crywalker).

I hired producers to help me bring the vision to life, and three camera guys. I saw myself as the creative director. Yes, it was intense! It took all day long to shoot. We did takes and retakes until it felt just right. I was being quite the perfectionist, and in hindsight I did have a rigid mindset about it all. I wanted it to be fun and funny, and I was holding myself to a very high standard.

If you scroll deep into my Instagram, you can still find the fully produced video, complete with music, and you can see for yourself the White Walker share his "Luke Crywalker" Anti-Self, as well as his "Sugar Walker" Best Self. I loved the final product; I was *thrilled* with it, so we posted it on social media the next day.

When I woke up a few hours later and reached for my phone, it felt like Christmas morning. I just knew there were going to be tons of views, likes, and comments. With the massive popularity of *Game of Thrones*, I thought sure everyone was going to flock to this video and take the challenge for themselves.

Boy, did I miss the mark on this one.

I could barely believe my eyes: the video had a whopping 150 likes. I'm a *New York Times* bestselling author, I'd architected this genius piece of content, and I was expecting it to go viral. I believed *Game of Thrones* fans were going to come across it and think it was just brilliant. Alas, crickets. Nothing. And all told, forty-six weeks after I posted the video, it's received 583 likes and 20 comments. Because of the video, I received four new followers. With the money I'd spent on the production as well as the money to advertise and boost the post, that's approximately $600 per new follower. I mean, come on! Epic fail. I was so bummed out.

I had been so focused on this vision in my head, and I was so convinced that it was going to take off, that I couldn't laugh about it at the time. I had a rigid mindset about it from the get-go, but what I needed to do was relax and have a laugh.

Something I've since come to learn about social media is that I can spend two seconds posting a shirtless photo of myself on the beach and get 31,042 likes, 936 comments, and 2,440 new followers, but something that requires a ton of thought and planning might not move the needle at all. Go figure.

The bottom line is this: in life, we have to experiment, take risks, and know that not everything we try is going to work. And when something doesn't work, in addition to finding the lesson within it, we've got to have at least a little fun with it . . . and realize it's not serious. When this White Walker story came back to me the other day, I wrote it down and then asked a friend to read it. He called me immediately afterward, and we both just started cracking up. It was that kind of thing where you're laughing so hard that it's just silent, with no sound coming out at all, and your abs hurt afterward. Even now, I have to chuckle when I think about how seriously I took that whole thing, and how horribly it flopped. Obviously, I've relaxed my mindset!

ARE YOU RIGID OR RELAXED?

Take a look at the comparison below between the negative FORCE of a rigid mindset and the positive FORCE of a relaxed mindset, and begin to think about how they might be affecting your thinking, especially as it pertains to the areas of your life you want to improve.

Try to think of this objectively, as if you were observing your thoughts and behavior as an outsider. I say this because especially when it comes to rigidity, it's sometimes tough to recognize in ourselves. But by this point in the chapter, I'm guessing you have been able to see areas in which you have some rigid ideas that need to relax. We have all been rigid from time to time, and it's good to be able to recognize how it can keep us stuck in the obstacle, unable to see or act on the opportunities.

Rigid:	Relaxed:
• Having a "my way or the highway" mentality.	• Taking a calm approach, willing to take a deep breath.
• Right fighting—needing to be right in every exchange/have the last word.	• Taking time to make others feel heard and seen.
• Believing that the way you've always done things is the only way to do them.	• Accepting life on life's terms instead of trying to dictate life.
	• Willing to ask, "Is it going to matter five years from now?"

EXERCISE

Take a look at this chart to see some real-life examples of a rigid mindset versus a relaxed mindset.

RIGID MINDSET	RELAXED MINDSET
This is the only way to do it.	I'm open to collaborating with others on the best possible way.
An argument isn't over until I've proven my point.	Every disagreement represents an opportunity to learn or grow.
I'm the parent; do as you're told.	I'm willing to be patient and work together with you.
I'm right. You're wrong.	It's not about who's right.

Now, fill in some examples of your own rigid mindset, especially as they relate to decisions you need to make in your life currently. Next, think about what the relaxed mindset version of those thoughts could be. Finally, what is a decision you could make based on that relaxed mindset?

RIGID MINDSET	RELAXED MINDSET	DECISION

My overall goal is to help you arrive at your One Decision that will be your first step toward a better life. To that end, I'd like you to look at the chart you filled in above and think about how your rigid mindset might be keeping you from making decisions that lead to a better life. In other words, how is your rigid mindset keeping you focused on the obstacles?

Write your thoughts below.

_____

_____

_____

_____

_____

Now, if you were to adopt a relaxed mindset instead, what are some opportunities that you can see that you couldn't before?

_____

_____

_____

_____

_____

Based on the opportunities you are seeing now that you are choosing a relaxed mindset, what is a decision you could make?

_____

_____

_____

_____

_____

Are you ready to take some form of action? Or are you at peace with things as they are? Write your answers here:

_____

_____

_____

_____

_____

NEXT UP IN THE FORCE . . .

As we make our way through the FORCE, I hope you are carrying with you the insights you've gained from each letter in the acronym thus far. Again, if you use them correctly, the positive FORCEs can propel you toward a better life, a life in which you recognize opportunities rather than stay stuck in obstacle after obstacle. Just as in *Star Wars*, the FORCE can be used for good or evil. Now that you're getting to pull back the veil and discover the ways in which these powerful FORCEs are already at play, you can wield them with purpose to create the life you truly desire.

And speaking of purpose, in the next chapter, you're going to discover how clarifying your purpose is the ultimate antidote to confusion. Are you *confused* by that statement? Turn the page to see what I mean!

8

FORCE

CONFUSED PURPOSE OR CLARIFIED PURPOSE

Have you ever been trying to make a decision, but your brain seems to go into hyperdrive, zooming from one thought or emotion to another, to the point that you don't even know which end is up? Maybe you imagine the potential outcomes (good, bad, and ugly), or obsess about doing the "right" thing, or worry about what people in your life think you should do. You might swing from one end of the pendulum and back again until you pretty much want to pull all your hair out. Ahhhh! It can be beyond infuriating. So, what do we do? Maybe we decide *not* to decide. Or perhaps we decide, but then constantly second-guess the decision. Or maybe we crawl back into bed and hide under the sheets and just give up.

So, what's the feeling causing all of this? Drumroll please . . . it's confusion! And I know you've felt it, because we all have. And I'll fully admit, this FORCE is often my Achilles' heel. I get myself all kinds of worked up and confused on the regular, so I can completely relate to this feeling.

Trying to make a decision while we're in a state of confusion not only is difficult but can be very stressful. A "confusion" mindset can make us feel overwhelmed and helpless and can cause a ton of anxiety. When we find ourselves overthinking or overanalyzing any situation, that's an example of confusion. If we obsessively go over what was said, or if we keep researching something on the internet over and over without landing on a conclusion—that's because we've created confusion in our minds. When we find ourselves seeking multiple opinions, or opinions from people who are not well versed in the topic at hand, and talking about it with everyone in our lives, that's what can occur when we're living in confusion. Some might refer to it as paralysis by analysis.

The need to people please is another example of how confusion can manifest itself in our lives. We think it's going to mean so much and feel so good to please another person, but it's never really enough. This might be characterized as when we have a really hard time saying no to anyone in our lives, and we put the needs and desires of others, even those with whom we are not very close, above our own. None of these confused feelings are coming from our Best Self, as you might imagine, and they certainly do not lead us toward making decisions from an authentic place within us.

THE POSITIVE FORCE: CLARIFIED PURPOSE

The solution when we are feeling confused and overwhelmed is to clarify our purpose. This requires exploration and curiosity. When we're confused about our next move, it's often because we don't know our purpose in that particular scenario; we haven't yet figured out how our Best Self aligns within it.

You see, confusion can only exist where there is no *purpose*. This is where relying on your decision team is hugely helpful, because you're asking people who have specific experience or wisdom about the decision you are trying to make and who can help you realign with your purpose. Once you have purpose, you have clarity and thus are no longer in a state of confusion.

I have felt confused within my career at various points in my life. It happens mostly when I've gotten focused on people liking me, or some other "surface" motivation that simply doesn't matter, instead of being focused on my *purpose*. My purpose isn't to be liked. My purpose is to help others. Every time I start a new project or endeavor by setting my sights on the end result, instead of my purpose (which we've all done from time to time), there always comes a point when I feel utterly confused. But when I take the time to remind myself of who I am, to sync back up with my Best Self, I can get back on course.

Life can get really confusing when you start doing things that don't bring you joy or happiness. You might feel like you're just clocking in, and maybe you're productive, but you're not fulfilled. It's unsettling. It can also manifest itself within relationships; for example, if we're in an unhealthy relationship that doesn't align with our purpose of having a loving, meaningful relationship, then we can feel distraught. The reason we feel distraught is that it runs contrary to our desire for a fulfilling relationship. Hence, we feel stuck, which leads to confusion about what to do. But if we decide to use it as an opportunity to clarify our purpose, then we realize that we deserve better. That could then lead to couples therapy, setting more boundaries, breaking up or divorcing, getting a restraining order; whatever it is, that decision can lead to aligning with our purpose. Settling for too long creates confusion.

Even in terms of our social life, confusion can be a real problem. If your purpose is to connect with friendships, and you're at a bar and everyone's drunk, but you don't drink, then what is your purpose for being there? If you don't want to party in the same way they do, then what's your purpose? Sure, you may spend time with friends, and I'm not saying you can't spend time with a bunch of drunks—to each their own! I just think this is a helpful indicator you can use to discover why you might feel confused. A great method to get yourself out of feeling self-conscious or as if you don't belong somewhere is to check in with yourself on your purpose. You can just pause and ask yourself, "What is my reason for being here?" and then use the answer to that question to inspire you to be your Best Self in that situation. Anytime in life that we don't have shared or aligned purpose with those in our various circles, feelings of confusion can arise. As we reinvent and shift our lives, our purpose evolves, and our job is to make sure every area of our life stays aligned with our purpose.

We can also feel confused about our purpose when things begin to change around us unexpectedly. We can't always predict what's going to happen. As I write this, the whole world has been thrust into a state of confusion in the middle of the COVID-19 pandemic. I've worked with plenty of folks whose lives have been upended, and their feelings of confusion are overwhelming right now. But here's the thing: even when things change around you, it doesn't change who you are. You cannot control the event, but you *can* control how you respond to it. You might need to change how you "do life," and it might even change how you interact with others, but it does not change your Best Self.

This is why taking time to clarify our purpose is so important.

In my own life, I can tell you, I've experienced a lot of changes, and my fair share of confusion as well. I had all this momentum building in the public speaking arena, and I was (finally!) starting to enjoy public speaking. It was super rewarding to get my message out there in a new way. But in light of the pandemic, public speaking isn't exactly an option. But rather than living in the obstacle-minded state of confusion, I returned to my purpose. I knew I had a message to share that was going to be more helpful to people than ever before, so I went about discovering another way to accomplish that. I have now shifted to virtual global empowerment groups and Facebook Live sessions, and though there's no monetary gain, I still get to help people. I get to keep doing it, just in a different way.

The same goes for my rehab CAST Centers. The heartbeat of it is the same; we are still providing help to people who need it. It's just that the business model had to change, and in fact this has become a big opportunity for us to reach even more people. We now have a new online treatment service that allows people to get treatment from the comfort of their home. Before, a stay-at-home mom or a mom with young kids couldn't leave her children to have treatment. Now she can. Or an executive who works twelve hours a day, instead of having to come to our offices for treatment, can do it from home. This crisis has provided us with an opportunity to help more people and expand our business. And the reason we have been able to adapt in this way is that we clarified our purpose, saw the opportunity, and made a decision to pivot.

Solutions and options became clear for me when I re-centered and zeroed in on the purpose for why we're running the rehab, and why I'm engaging with the public. My purpose is to be myself, and to help others to find the freedom to do the same. When I'm living in that headspace, everything feels crystal clear.

AUSTIN'S JOURNEY TO CLARIFY HIS PURPOSE

I want to share a coaching session I recently did so that you can see what confusion looks like in action. Very often, we don't *real-*

ize we are confused until we start to talk everything out that we've been thinking. Once we say it out loud, or write it all down, we begin to see that we've been cycling around the same thoughts but not making any progress.

Austin and I sat down to discuss his job, which he'd been in for seven years. He's only thirty-one years old, but lately he's felt paralyzed and unable to make a decision about his next move. Here's how that conversation played out.

Austin started, "Well, I studied Japanese language and business management in college. At the time, I was really into Japanese culture and anime. I wanted to study abroad in Japan and thought maybe I would have some international business opportunity. It was an awesome journey and I wouldn't trade it for anything, but that kind of faded. When I graduated college, I immediately got offered this job working for this custom furniture company. I went for it, and it's been a really great job. But it's not really a passion by any means, and I'm starting to feel like if I don't make a change, it's just going to get harder and harder. Not that it's not possible, but it's already feeling kind of tough to break out of my current situation."

I asked, "How long have you felt like this?"

Immediately, albeit a little sheepishly, he answered, "I knew from the very beginning that it wasn't really the direction I wanted to go. I was twenty-four when I started there." He paused, drew in a breath, and began his justification. "But the money was good, and there was a lot of freedom with the job. I was able to travel a lot, and I was putting money in the bank every month. But about a year ago, I was ready to move from New York to California; I missed the weather, missed my family. So they offered me this position in L.A."

I replied, "From twenty-four to thirty years old, during that period of six years, have you ever felt like *yes, this is my passion*?"

He said, "I've never felt like it was my passion. I felt like it was good experience, it was good money, it was a ticket to see the world, to travel. I mean, it was kind of smooth sailing for a while, honestly, the easy route," and then his eyes sort of glazed a bit, and he stared into the distance, thinking.

I asked, "So, why do you think you settled?"

"That's a good question. I've always kind of struggled with my direction. What do I want to do? Like if I were to really go for my deepest, wildest dreams. And sometimes the easy way is just to say, *I can make this work*."

"What does work mean to you? What is the meaning of having a job?" I asked.

"Well, you spend a lot of time with your job, so . . ." His voice trailed off.

I leaned forward in my chair a bit and said, "Is it not important to you to have purpose?"

"Oh," he said, "sure, it really is important to me to have purpose."

"But you've been going on seven years now and you haven't really had purpose in your work. How much time and energy are you putting toward making the change?" I asked.

"I mean, it's been tough because my job is really demanding. And I enjoy my downtime, like the gym, social time here and there, so it's hard to really put any energy into it. I'm trying to figure out the balance like how much time I need to focus on finding a new job and how much effort I need to keep in my current job to make—"

I interrupted: "What I'm hearing you say, though, is 'I'm unhappy in my job, however, I need downtime to hang out with my friends.' Is that right?"

Nodding, he said, "Yep."

"And what is blocking you—what is the story you're telling yourself?"

"There's probably some fear and trepidation in there. And also, I don't want to say laziness, but it's hard to motivate sometimes," he replied.

"Could it be you just don't want to work?" I asked.

Quick to answer, he said, "No, that's not it. I would love to have a job that I'm passionate about and I enjoy putting energy in, like giving it my all. You know what I mean? I think it's because I'm not convinced I know what I want to do."

"So, could it be 'I don't know what I want to do, and until I do, I can't make a decision'?"

"That's pretty accurate," he said, then gathered his thoughts for a moment and said, "I have always loved anything related to airplanes. But I never pursued that."

I said, "This has been your career for seven years. You're thirty-one years old, so that's 23 percent of your life. And really for half of your adult life, at least, you've been in a career that's not totally satisfying you," I said.

After a brief pause, he said, "Yeah, that's correct."

I said, "There's a story you're telling yourself, which I believe is the reason you're not learning something new, getting inspired on a Saturday night instead of watching a movie. They're both entertaining, but one brings you more toward new ideas and possibilities, and one will just entertain you. It seems to me you've been in a pattern of work is work and you haven't had a blending of lifestyle with career."

"Right, it's been separate," he replied.

"I find that a lot of people, when their work and their lifestyle are separate, they never want to talk about work, and when they have to go to work, it's like 'Ugh, I have to go to work.'"

He said, "That's what people who don't love their job say."

"Correct, and then there are those people who have a job and lifestyle that are kind of blended. Their life inspires their work and their work inspires their life. There's this relationship between the two," I said.

His eyes lighting up for the first time, Austin said, "Yeah, I want that."

I asked, "So, how do we get that?"

Without skipping a beat, he said, "I think it would be really helpful if I had a road map from my current position to my dream job. Like what do I need to do . . ."

I interjected: "But, listen. I'd say I've been in my dream job for, like, seventeen years, and I've done a thousand different jobs. The journey has always been the destination. There's no 'I've made it. I'm in my job!'"

"And I'm into so many things—geography, maps, culture, languages, travel, like, I'm passionate about that stuff. I think that's also something that holds me back too. I get *so* confused in all of it."

"Because you've had a story about how you studied Japanese and thought you were going to be doing that, and you thought—

'I spent so much time and energy pursuing something, and I didn't . . .'"

Austin jumped in, now talking at light speed: "And I could go back to school, but I would have to take out a loan, and then I would lose my social life—I tell myself all these things, but maybe I just need to pull the trigger. I don't know."

I said, "It sounds like you've paralyzed yourself."

Pointing his finger and nodding fervently, he said, "I do feel paralyzed sometimes, I really do. That's a good way to explain it!"

"And have you ever felt indecisive in this way before?" I asked.

"Yeah, but not to this degree. When I was younger, things didn't feel as final and heavy. I didn't have as much responsibility," he said.

I asked, "And how does it feel when you're paralyzed?"

Thoughtfully considering his answer, he said, "I wish I knew what to do to make it work, to make a change."

"Do you think you're depressed?" I asked.

"Probably a little bit, yeah. I definitely went through some depression last year. At the time, I thought, 'Wow, *this* is what depression feels like.'"

As a follow-up, I asked, "Have you been on meds ever?"

"No, I don't know if I'm really open to it. I feel like there is a way out without having to take meds. Unless there were medications that would help me be more motivated, help me, like, actually do something rather than feel paralyzed," he replied.

I said, "To me, you're talking about a road map to the next job where—in my opinion—it's a road map to more purpose and meaning. And *out* of that will come the job. Because you're not going to be open to opportunities if your brain's not open to opportunities.

Opportunities are probably even running around you; you have no ability to see them right now."

"Right," he said, taking that in.

"Are you scared of rejection? Or that you can't do it? Or that you aren't deserving?" I asked.

Shaking his head slightly, he said, "I feel like I'm deserving, but maybe sometimes I feel like I'm not good enough. But when I ask myself, 'Do you really think you're not good enough?' No, I don't think that."

"But you're just behaving that way," I pointed out.

"Yeah."

"Your actions are telling me that you're avoiding getting what you want out of this life because of excuses. I simply don't believe that the reason you're not choosing your passion and purpose and meaning in life is because of laundry!" We both laughed out loud.

I continued, "Or the gym, or the rest of your list of excuses! There are decisions you have to make if you actually want to have that purpose and meaning be integrated so you're inspired in your career. You believe it has to be this process or that procedure. But you did that and it hasn't given you the results that you totally want. Right?"

"Right," he said.

"Yeah, but that's a belief system you've created. What I do for a living, there's not even a name for it. I'm a life coach, before that it was interventions, before that I was a counselor, I owned a rehab, I work with pop stars navigating breakups and relationships. It's completely all over the map, right?" Austin was nodding. I continued, "From people who want to kill themselves to people who want to get a better job. And if I had the belief that I am not qualified enough or I'm not trained enough, or I don't have a PhD in clinical psychology or all these things, then I wouldn't be doing what I'm doing. Because I would be believing all those stories. And you have a list of stories that are not true. You're saying, 'Yeah, but . . . I'm not qualified enough. Yeah, but . . . I haven't worked in the industry before. Yeah, but . . . that means I need to go back to college.' You haven't even tried," I said.

"You're right," he said.

"I think you're viewing a career as a story. You're creating a story to believe that it's got to be a 'Dream Job,' and you have to have a 'Road Map.' So, we have to create a new story that isn't impossible to achieve," I said as he nodded with understanding. "A friend of mine, his dream job was to be a veterinarian. He became a veterinarian; then he became an attorney! Then he changed from being an attorney and now he's an addiction professor at UCLA," I said.

"I've always been like that too."

"But that's fun! That's good! So, how could we turn excuses into empowerments? Give me one of your go-to excuses."

"I'm tired. The gym. Laundry. Trying to eat right. Those are just things I put my energy into. After I do those things, I've left myself no energy."

"So, what you're telling me is your gym workout is more important than your passion projects in your life?"

Looking slightly stricken, he replied, "I've probably prioritized that, yeah."

"So, fast-forward a year from now, same date, same time, you could be in the same spot you are right now, or worse."

"Which I don't want."

"But you don't want to do what you need to do. Your number one problem is you lack a sense of purpose in your career. You need to learn to get curious, start asking about other jobs, other pathways: 'How'd you do that? What was that like, and do you like it?' Even interactions with friends are opportunities to ask questions. Because right now, you're only thinking about traditional routes and that just sounds awful—you're thinking more about the obstacles in front of you than the purpose behind overcoming them," I said.

We both laughed, and he said, "Right, I agree."

"Your brain knows the answer, you know. That road map you've been talking about, you already have it inside you. Your default has been to say, 'I don't know. It's too late, I don't know how to do it.' So, we have got to create new neural pathways in your brain. What would start to get you fired up?"

"I need to start finding opportunities," he said.

"Okay," I said. "You're going to *create* opportunities. Talk to me about what you can do this week that would inspire you to get you in a different mindset. What is going to recharge yourself so that you're actually in the flow of who you authentically are and what you love. What's going to get you fired up?" I asked.

"It's hard to say. I mean, I do enjoy hiking, going to the beach, that kind of stuff, but I don't know if that's going to inspire me, because I do that stuff all the time, and here I am, just as confused as ever," he said.

"But look at the optic you're looking through. When you go hiking, you're not thinking about how inspired and creative you are.

You're not thinking, 'Look at that tree. It's in the shape of a triangle and I'm going to sketch that when I leave.' The way to find your purpose isn't to focus on currency; it's to focus on passion," I said. And because Austin and I were sitting in my living room, which I've put a lot of energy into decorating, I just waved my hand around and said, "So, we're in this room right now; we're in my house. Look around; what in this room could create passion or inspiration for you?"

"I actually love the design of your place, the furniture, the finishings, the artwork, definitely inspiring to me. I would love to have the means to create this sort of thing myself," he said.

"Yeah, so it's possible for you to create those means if you believe it's possible to create those means," I said.

"I believe it's possible, but I find myself in the way of that possibility," he said.

"You're on the fence, right? Part of you thinks it's possible, part of you thinks it isn't?" I asked.

"Right, like there's something inside of me that's unable to answer this question, like what can motivate me, what can inspire me? I'm like digging for something but coming up empty-handed," he said.

"I think you're a little depressed," I said.

He replied, "Probably." After a pause, he said, "It probably wouldn't be a bad idea to have a proper psychological assessment."

"Have you gone to therapy before?" I asked.

"No."

"Never? My God, you're missing out. It's, like, the best," I said.

"It's actually been one of my New Year's resolutions, to go to therapy and try to get some clarity on what's holding me back, why I'm having this paralysis. I really can't put my finger on it."

"I actually think *that's* the decision you need to make," I replied.

"To start going to therapy?" he asked.

"Yes," I said.

Thinking about that for a moment, he then said, "I think that's a good start for sure."

I said, "I think that if you went to therapy, you would have huge benefits. I'm thinking more coaching-style, where you talk about 'what's the next step, let's get to it.' But I actually don't think your biggest problem is the job," I said.

Austin nodded slowly, moved around in his seat a bit, and said, "No, probably not."

"I think you're just unhappy."

"Yeah. I am," he said.

"So, you made your decision. You have the first part of your road map. I can't wait to see where you go next," I said.

"Me neither," Austin replied.

Are you able to see how Austin was getting caught up in the confusion? Every time we started talking about passions and inspirations, which would normally lead to a larger conversation about purpose, he kept returning to process. He thought he needed to focus on process, but he could never figure out what that process was for him, what steps he was going to follow through on. So, he'd return to the negative thoughts about himself, his capabilities, and he'd just remain stuck, cycling around the same thoughts and not going anywhere. His confusion always kept him focused on the obstacles. It became clear to me that he had some things he needed to work through, and some depression to manage, and then it would be easier for his brain to start clarifying his purpose. But it started by talking it out and recognizing the confusion for what it was.

Just a couple weeks after we sat down for this conversation, he checked into CAST Centers and started working on his depression and anxiety. Once he got to the root of where his depression was coming from, and he learned some coping tools for managing it, the fog began to lift. He was able to see that his work and his lifestyle didn't have to be completely separated. And he gave himself permission to more fully explore his passions. He began living as his Best Self and then slowly started making decisions for his life from that place, rather than from a place of depression and confusion.

Then the universe dealt Austin an unexpected card, as it sometimes does. He got laid off from his job. But instead of thinking of this as an obstacle—as many of us might in this situation—he immediately approached the turn of events as a huge opportunity, and saw that this was his chance to explore and clarify his true life's purpose. He knew it was time for a reinvention. Ever since he'd been a kid, airplanes had fascinated him, and for years he'd been telling himself that it was too late for him to do anything about it. But now, with his fresh take on life, he knew it was time to stop telling himself that story, and to take real steps toward living in alignment with his purpose. As I write this, Austin is working toward becoming a pilot. I couldn't be happier for him.

MANAGING DEPRESSION CAN RELIEVE CONFUSION

When depression or anxiety is a factor for you, as it was for Austin, addressing it head-on can help you achieve a whole new level of clarity. Seeking therapy might just be your One Decision that will catapult you into a better life, because it can help you remove mental obstacles that have been keeping you in a state of confusion. You'll be more able to access and connect with your purpose, because you aren't first having to jump over that hurdle of depression.

Right now, let's take a look at the overview on confused versus clarified purpose and ask yourself this question: Are you dealing with any level of confusion in specific areas of your life? Start to think about that, but don't write anything down yet.

Confused Purpose:

- Overthinking situations to the point of feeling helpless, overwhelmed.

- Out of indecision, getting stuck in inaction.

- Seeking too many opinions, and losing touch with gut instincts.

- Potentially becoming co-dependent.

- People pleasing.

Clarified Purpose:

- Asking ourselves about the reason we're making a decision one way or another.

- Realizing that some decisions are not about our "life's purpose" and that we might just have a role to play in certain situations.

- Understanding/discovering our purpose in any situation.

- Working with a decision team to help realign with your purpose.

CONFUSION TORNADOES

I was out to dinner with my friend Amy not too long ago, and she was trying to make what she felt was a pretty big decision on behalf of her child. She's a single mom, and her son had been struggling in school. Despite her attempts to work it out with the administration, she felt like it was a losing battle, and her son wasn't going to thrive in that specific environment. She wanted to put him into a new school or homeschool him. When she brought it up, it was interesting to see how her whole demeanor changed. By the time she finished telling me the high-level details of the situation, she was practically holding on to the table like she was bracing herself. Pointing it out, I asked, "It looks like you're holding on for dear life right now. Are you okay?"

She looked down and saw that every muscle in her upper body was tense, to the point that she could clearly see the veins in her hands. She laughed slightly and said, "I was gripping the steering wheel so hard the other day that my fingers all went numb. It's like I feel as if I'm going to get blown away by a tornado."

I knew she'd grown up in Oklahoma, right in the heart of Tornado Alley, and I felt like this metaphor might be helpful in identifying what was going on in her decision-making process. "Do you have a pen and any kind of paper?" I asked.

She dug both out of her purse and started to hand them to me.

"They're for you. I want you to write something."

"Okay . . . ," she said, looking at me skeptically.

"Think about that tornado you've been bracing for every time you're thinking of this big decision that you need to make. Now, write out the most prominent words or phrases that have been swirling in your head every time you try to make this decision."

She tapped the pen on her lip for a second and then started to write. Then she read them out loud: "His future, my mom's opinion, lifestyle change, what if I'm wrong, bad mom, money."

When she was finished, I said, "Take a look at that. How does that make you feel?"

"It's causing anxiety for sure. These thoughts just keep swishing by, each in a fast rotation, over and over. My heart is kind of racing. Sometimes when I'm thinking like this, it feels like a butterfly is in my chest, my heart is beating so erratically."

"And do you think that this process will help you arrive at a decision of any kind?"

Shaking her head and rolling her eyes upward, she replied, "Not a good one, that's for sure. But I can't get my thoughts in order. I'm confusing myself into oblivion."

"Right. So it seems like you have the committee in your head all talking at once." She started nodding and smiling, and I went on, "And you're cycling through them over and over."

"Yes. And I've talked to so many people, Mike. I've literally asked everyone in my life for their opinion on this. And experts. And more experts. Facebook groups. You name it, I've sought advice from them. But everyone thinks something different. I can't get a consensus, so now all those opinions are just part of the tornado of confusion," she said.

"Okay, but of everyone you've spoken to, is there anyone who knows you, knows your son, and is an expert in the area of education?" I asked.

She thought about that, mentally going through the list of people she'd spoken to, and said, "Well, not really, no. They either know us or they're some kind of specific expert, either on homeschooling or on private school."

"Got it. So I think one of the first things that will help you is to talk to someone, and maybe it's a child psychologist who can evaluate him and then offer an opinion on the best type of school for him. Because all of these opinions from people are just serving to further confuse you, it seems. Would you agree?"

"Yes, for sure. That's a good idea," she said.

"But let me also ask you this: What is your purpose in this decision? When it comes to your son's schooling, what is *your* purpose?"

"Hmmm. I think I've kind of lost sight of my specific purpose. I mean, clearly, I want to do right by my son. But I've been debating about whether my new role is to be his educator, and what that life would look like. I mean, I have to work, so how would I also educate him? And how do I know for sure I'm doing right by him regardless of what I choose? I'm at a loss," she said.

"Write down three words or phrases that come to mind when you think about your purpose within your son's education."

She started to write, stopped, started to write again, paused, and then got going. Then she picked it up and read out loud, "Make sure he feels heard, instill a love of learning, enjoy life together." And then she sighed deeply.

"How does that feel?" I asked.

"Better. A lot better. It simplifies things," she said.

"Do you think if you focused on those thoughts rather than the committee of voices and all that confusion that you'd be more likely to arrive at a decision?" I asked.

"I do. Yes, because I think I'd sort of lost sight of my overall goals, the things I wanted most for him. I was caught up in everyone's agendas," she replied.

"So, look at your tornado words again. How do you feel looking at them?" I asked.

"Not so bad, actually. I feel almost like I'm watching it from above now. It's there, but it can't get to me. If that makes sense? I don't feel threatened like I did before," she said.

"And you're not holding on to the table like you're about to be blown away anymore, so that's an improvement," I said, and we both laughed.

MOVING FROM CONFUSED PURPOSE TO CLARIFIED PURPOSE

Are you feeling confused about a decision you need to make? Or perhaps you're feeling confused in the area you most want to improve in your life, and it's causing indecision? Take a look at this chart with real-life examples of a confused purpose versus a clarified purpose.

CONFUSED PURPOSE	CLARIFIED PURPOSE
I have to make the *right* decision. If I don't, I'll suffer with regrets.	There is no right or wrong, only aligned or not. I'm going to focus on my purpose rather than the outcome, and then let it go.
Everyone is telling me something different; I don't know how to decide.	I will ask someone on my One Decision team to remind me of my purpose, and I'll lean on that person to help me act within that purpose.
I don't know why I'm doing this anymore; I feel lost and unmotivated.	I know who I am, and I will let that truth guide me and motivate me.

EXERCISE

Now, think about a decision you could make, or need to make. In the empty chart below, write down any thoughts that reflect a feeling of confusion around that decision under "Confused Purpose." Then think about how you can realign with your purpose, and with who you are, and write those thoughts under "Clarified Purpose."

CONFUSED PURPOSE	CLARIFIED PURPOSE

Now, from that clarified purpose state of mind, what are some opportunities you have that you perhaps couldn't see when you were feeling confused?

_____

_____

_____

_____

_____

_____

Finally, focusing on those opportunities, and within that clarified purpose mindset, what is a decision you could make that would better your life in some way?

_____

_____

_____

_____

_____

OUT OF CONFUSION AND INTO YOUR PURPOSE

Whenever you feel like you don't know why you're somewhere or why you're doing a job that doesn't feel good, or needing to tap back into inspiration, or just confused about how to move forward, clarifying your purpose is the medicine to heal your confusion.

Up next, you're going to work on the final letter of the FORCE, which is *E*, and it will help you see how your feelings can sometimes get in the way of the facts. Here we go!

9

FORCE

EMOTIONAL REASONING OR
EVIDENCE-BASED REASONING

Emotions can be extremely powerful. If you've ever been in the grips of a debilitating anxiety attack, overcome with blinding anger, or brought to your knees in sadness, you know just what I mean. On the other hand, if you've ever felt like you were floating on a cloud of joy or were filled to overflowing with gratitude or laughed so hard you cried, then you also have experienced the power of emotions. We humans are highly emotional beings, and we've evolved this way for many reasons. Emotions bind us together in relationships and communities, they help us accomplish societal goals, they push us to create new solutions and technology, and they protect us and motivate us. But given too much free rein, emotions can also cause us to make irrational, inauthentic decisions that can harm us and those around us.

Balancing our emotions is an important skill, specifically when it comes to decision making.

The way to know if we are out of balance is when we begin to lose sight of the difference between what we feel to be true and what actually is true. If we're making decisions that are based in feeling, that is emotional reasoning, whereas if we are making decisions that are based in actual, verifiable evidence, that is evidence-based reasoning. When we are reasoning with emotion, we believe that feelings *are* facts. When we are using evidence-based reasoning, we are able to recognize and then set aside the emotions and lean primarily on the evidence when making decisions. This prevents us from deciding on something that isn't in our best interest because it was based on a short-term, fleeting emotion.

Anyone who has let their feelings be their primary navigation system throughout life might struggle at first with being able to shift from emotion to evidence. But it's an incredibly rewarding shift to make, because it allows you to own and shape your emotions, rather than constantly reacting to whatever occurs in life. You don't have to live wondering who is going to hurt you next, or whether the events of each day are going to batter and bruise you or uplift and fulfill you. Instead, your happiness is coming from a place *within* you, from your Best Self, rather than from external factors. It can be an empowering process, and can give you the freedom to take control over your emotions and make sound decisions that give you peace, regardless of the outcome.

I DON'T *FEEL* LIKE IT . . .

So much of our growth and progress as individuals occurs when we step outside our comfort zone and push ourselves to do something even when we don't "feel" like it. If we let our feelings dictate all of our actions, we would likely never evolve. So when we say to ourselves, "I'm not going to do the work in this book today, because I don't feel like it," or "I'm not going to work out today; I just don't feel like it," or "I'm not going to fix my kid's lunch, because I don't feel like it," we need to then ask ourselves whether our feeling matters more than what we're sacrificing. Nine times out of ten, we will *feel* better if we just do it anyway. Just like when we're growing physically, and we experience growing pains, evolving as a person also involves feeling uncomfortable from time to time. You can't always go by feelings; you must return to the facts.

ROCCO'S EMOTIONALLY DRIVEN DECISIONS

It's not always easy to realize or identify when we are using emotional reasoning. Especially when our emotions have been in the driver seat for our day-to-day life for an extended period of time, it's challenging to recognize this kind of pattern. Again, when we are steeped in emotional reasoning, we confuse feelings with facts. We believe if we feel something, then it is real. But what I've found is when we begin unpacking the motivations for our actions, we can start to see where we've let emotions, rather than evidence, drive our decision making.

In one of my recent coaching sessions, that's exactly what happened. When Rocco and I sat down, neither of us had any idea where this conversation might go. He has always been interested in self-help topics and has done a lot of work on himself over the years, so he was very open and willing to explore any potential opportunities for improving himself.

To get things going, we started off by going through the assessment of the various areas of his life, and he'd been rating each area pretty neutral—could be better, but not an urgent need for change. But when we got to "family life," he immediately rated it a 1. Here's what happened next.

"Why do you rate your family life so low? Who in specific are you referring to?" I asked.

"My mom passed away three years ago, so it's really my relationship with my dad. He is going through some major issues, and I guess it is seeping through to me," he replied.

"Okay, got it. What about your emotional health?" I asked.

"I'd rate it a 9 or 10. I feel 100 percent uplifted. It could always be better, of course," he replied, with a big confident smile on his face.

"But you're genuinely happy. That's great," I said.

"Yes, I am," he said, shifting a bit on the couch.

"Okay. And romantic relationships? How are those?" I asked.

"I don't have any intimate relationships right now; I just got out of a serious one. I'd rate this area a 5. I can see the red flags better than I did before, and see the people who are the energy I want in my life now," he said, clearly having thought about this before.

"And where in your life do you feel like you've been making decisions that don't feel good to you?"

That last question resonated, and his speech quickened as he said, "I guess I don't feel great about my decisions in relationships. A recurring problem is I always seem to attract a certain type of person into my life. My Al-Anon coach told me I'm 'Mr. Fix Broken Girls or Broken People,' because I always try to accept people in my life who are going through shit." (In case you haven't heard of Al-Anon Family Groups before, they offer a program of recovery to help families and friends of problem drinkers recover from the impacts of a loved one's drinking.)

"So, you're attracted to people who need you to fix them?" I asked.

"I'm not always the one to fix them, but yes. I get attracted to that because of my mom and that's what I saw in my last relationship," he replied.

"When you say your mom . . . I'm remembering now she struggled with addiction. And how old was she when she died?"

"She died at fifty, of an overdose of fentanyl and cocaine," he said.

"And so you grew up in chaos?" He started nodding, so I continued, "It became normal for you to have to take care of others? And that's how you found yourself in relationships?"

This struck a chord, and he began to tell his story. "Yes. In my childhood, I was nomadic. Moving place to place, woken up in the middle of the night to go play cards at my mom's friend's house. As an only child, I always had to make friends with people. I saw my mom overdose multiple times, not knowing what was going on at the time. My parents divorced when I was seven, and my mom started dating other people, even got engaged once, but it fell through. She lost our house, and we moved into an apartment. I started realizing that she was addicted to drugs. I moved in with my dad and things fell apart slowly but surely for my mom. She lost her biggest job of fifteen years; then she got another one and it was paying okay, and then she lost that. The addiction was taking a toll, and the quality of people she was spending time with kept getting lower and lower. At fifteen or sixteen years old, I told her to stop hanging out with white trash people. It seemed like she wanted to help them, but it just wasn't working."

Rocco's childhood story, unfortunately, is not uncommon. According to the National Survey on Drug Use and Health, one in eight children (which translates to 8.7 million kids in the United States) aged seventeen or younger lives in a household with at least one parent who has a substance use disorder.

I asked, "In your relationships, you end up with people who aren't healthy for you?"

With a bit of a frown, he said, "My last few have been extremely toxic."

"And is that similar to how it felt growing up?"

"Yeah, and actually my dad said, when he met my ex, that she reminded him of my mom, and I thought, 'Oh, he means all the good things,' but as the relationship went on, I realized it wasn't just the good things."

I said, "Talk to me about when you make a decision, like with your ex, how do your emotions affect your decisions? For example, the decision to be with her. Do you believe your emotions suddenly dictate everything?"

"Yes, totally. I felt like she was my world, my everything."

"Was that because it felt so good?" I asked.

Pausing briefly to consider this, he then said, "I was telling myself a story in my head. I was convincing myself for some reason. Even though I was extremely stressed and it seemed she could walk away at any minute."

"Okay, explain exactly what happened with your ex."

"We got together and I thought I fell in love the first night I met her. Everything was amazing."

I asked, "You thought to yourself, 'This is the woman I want to marry'?"

"Yes, for sure," he replied, remembering that night.

"And where were you when you met her?" I asked, curious to hear the details surrounding this love-at-first-sight encounter.

"At a nightclub," he said, laughing loudly.

"And were you sober? Was she?" I asked, also laughing a bit.

"She was drinking," he said.

"What were you doing?" I asked.

"Molly," he admitted.

"Ecstasy. Okay, so the night you met her you were on ecstasy. And you were convinced you loved her. But don't you love *everyone* on ecstasy?" I said. By now, we were both laughing pretty hard.

"Yeah, but not like I loved *her*, though," he said.

"And did you go home together?"

"Yes," he said.

"And did you leave the next day? Or what happened afterward?"

He said, "After that moment, we didn't spend a day apart for two . . . straight . . . years."

"Okay. And how long after meeting her did you propose?" I asked.

"A year and a half," he said.

"And during that year and a half, were there any fights between the two of you?"

"Oh, plenty of fights," he said with no hesitation, but also casting his eyes downward.

"A lot of fights?" I asked.

"Yeah. Never a fight that I picked, though. I was always the one on my heels saying to myself, 'How did we get into a fight here? I don't think this should be a fight.' I'm a communicative person. I'll be assertive with something I stand for, but I'll never cause a fight out of something that's silly. I'll never get overly upset. I'll remove myself from the situation, compose myself, and communicate it. But with her, if I got one less box of frozen rice it was 'You don't listen to me, you don't understand me,'" he said.

"So, knowing you had someone angry at you for grabbing one less box of rice, walk me through your decision to ask her to be your wife. How many fights did you get into?"

"Probably like twenty big ones," he said.

"Twenty. Okay. And how many small ones?"

"There was always something I was doing wrong, or she'd say, 'You're playing victim,' or she'd tell me, 'Be friends with these people,' and she was always questioning who I am. I thought it was her challenging me to be a better person and it felt like I was in love with her, and the story I told myself was to do everything for her, and I would justify it, thinking she was helping me grow," he said.

"You reasoned that because you loved her, that took precedence over everything, over the conflict, the fights?" I asked.

"I loved her so much I would justify *everything*," he said, with a bit of a different look about him. It seemed like he was starting to experience a new level of awareness.

"So, your emotional reasoning told you not to look at the red flags, not to look at what's best for you; it was just that you loved her so much it didn't matter what she did, right?" I asked.

Slowly nodding his head and leaning back in his seat, he said, "I remember saying to someone that she could cheat on me and I'd forgive her because I loved her so much," he replied.

"You used your emotions to justify everything?" I asked.

"Everything," he confirmed. He had a knowing smile on his face now, because he could see things more clearly with the benefit of hindsight.

"And you see that, right? You're smiling," I told him. We both laughed.

"It's funny because I'm a pretty logical person and I'm not this overly emotional. But now I'm realizing I was letting my emotions control everything because of the love I had for her," he said.

"It sounds like you ignored the evidence," I said.

Nodding again, he said, "Oh yeah. And everyone knew it. My Al-Anon coach, everyone."

"So why would that not happen again? Because it sounds like when love gets in your mind, you ignore the evidence."

"I feel like it's tied to seeing my mom go through all that stuff. So, with my girlfriend, I would say, 'Oh, this week she took Molly;

that's why she's acting this way.' Or I would justify it by thinking, 'She was raped, or had sexual abuse, and that's the reason that she would act like this. That's why she's running to the balcony and screaming help like I'm holding her hostage.' I justified why she was saying she was not happy. I'd always say to her, 'I'm not the person to make you happy. I'm your lover, here to love you, to be your person and help you with what I can help you with, but I can't help you with your happiness. That's something *you* have to do,'" he said.

"There's something I call the Boogeyman. What happened with your mom when you were growing up has created a story that you are hardwired to believe. And it's telling you that loving someone means tolerating their crazy. Or abuse. Or emotional abuse. Or neglect. Or all of it. That's what you learned growing up, and so you have believed that. But that's not a *true* story. That's just how you're hardwired. That's the narrative that haunts your adult life today. In order to take action to not let that Boogeyman take over, what decision do you need to make so that shifts for you?"

Thoughtfully, he said, "I think definitely I need more self-love and self-respect, and to put boundaries around what I will tolerate and what I won't. I shouldn't tolerate neglect or abuse or try to reason with those things because of a certain emotion I have for someone. If I see a red flag, I need to value myself more—practice more spirituality, go to a psychologist. To work on myself instead of trying to fix that other person. Someone said to me, if you get in a car accident, you need to go through physical therapy. I went through emotional and mental trauma with Mom being a drug addict for thirty-five years and I lived through twenty-two years of that. The emotional trauma I went through can't be healed with meditation and self-help books. I need to get that healed so that I can go back to a homeostasis, a state where I can accept actual love in my life," he said.

"Yeah, so you can be empowered for yourself. And so that the empowerment overrides your falling back into old patterns."

"Because I continue to do that all the time."

I said, "I think going to a therapist would be wonderful for you so that you can shift and find a new way to look at love, and attachment to love. You can make a decision to be proactive. Like you said, otherwise you kind of just repeat the pattern. I can get a recommendation for a therapist for you so you can make a decision to start your journey of healing. It sucks we can't just recognize what the problem is and cognitively go, 'Okay, I moved past that, and I'm good now.' And we think, 'I have to go work on this thing inside of myself?' But it's also the best thing we can do. We can decide to let the elements we want define our future, and those elements we don't want don't have to define our future. Have you been to therapy?"

"No, never," he said.

"And look how far you've come with no therapy!"

He smiled and said, "It's all been through self-help books and reading and research. To get to my reason why. And I've realized a lot of my identity, my mom was always super proud of me, *overly* proud, and my dad didn't show his pride. I wanted to make him proud but also earn the affection of my mom that was genuine. She got me things, and then would hold them over my head. But what I wanted was for my mom to be at my football games, mentally there, not on drugs, with the family, and with her sanity, clarity. I wanted her physically, mentally, spiritually, all there. And it seemed like I was trying to earn that love and affection, but also have my dad show pride. With my mom, she talked about me to everyone. It didn't seem genuine, because I just thought, 'How could you love me so much and be so proud of me, but you can't hold it together for me as your son?' "

And then he stopped. The silence was heavy with the weight of what he'd just said. He stared into space, thoughtful. And then I replied, "She couldn't."

Looking down at his hands, which were clasped together, he said, "Yeah."

"All of that. You need to be able to talk with someone and connect dots and heal that. Because here's the thing: it's a decision to heal your past so that your future is different."

He said, "Kind of set the intention to heal my past."

"Right? So that you can have a different reality," I said. "And so that you can start to make decisions that are evidence based, rather than emotionally based. Because, look, you can't actually fall in love with someone the minute you meet them, especially in a nightclub. You have to consider the evidence, look at the entire situation, ask yourself if there are other factors at play. The evidence you need to consider is that you can't actually get to know someone on an intimate level in those circumstances, and in that amount of time. You need to look at whether this person treats you with love too. What evidence is there that this is a healthy, positive relationship, for either of you? Rather than letting the powerful emotion of 'I'm in love with this person' lead you on a path, you want to consider the evidence as more important than the emotion."

He replied, "When you talk about evidence, I remember . . . she was actually telling me she didn't want to be with me, and I'd be like 'No, you're just upset.' But now in reality, no, she was communicating with me that she was not happy. But I was just letting my emotions run everything. I should've been like 'Oh, you don't want to be with me, you're not happy, then go!' "

I said, "Or maybe it's 'you're not what I need.' You didn't have a choice growing up, but you have a choice now. It's not about whether or not she wants to be with you. It's not healthy for *you*." And then I continued, "We know for starters it's probably not best to meet someone at a nightclub on ecstasy. I think that's the first step." We shared a good laugh over that simple truth.

Rocco started therapy the next week—his first decision leading him toward a better life. He'd already done so much work on himself through his own research and his willingness and curiosity about his behavior, and had developed such a keen awareness of how his past connected with his present decision making. Now he can choose to stop repeating harmful patterns, especially in his relationships.

When we first sat down, Rocco hadn't seen any urgent need in his emotional life, but once we started talking about his relationships and he connected the dots to see how he was using emotional reasoning, he experienced a critical shift. What changed? He looked at the *evidence*.

Instead of allowing the emotions to determine what was true, he let the evidence supersede what his emotions were telling him. We cannot feel our way to decisions that are in our best interest. Just because we feel something, that doesn't make it true. He *felt* that he was in love with someone who didn't care about him, who mistreated him, and who wasn't available for a real, authentic relationship. But when he took a step back and considered all the evidence, from how he'd been raised, to how they'd met, to how she'd told him time and again that she didn't want a relationship, he could see that his feelings were not the truth. And they certainly were not coming from his Best Self, or leading him toward a better life.

I spoke to Rocco recently to get an update, and he told me that he has gained such clarity about the ways he was making emotionally driven decisions. He said he's able to identify it and then stop himself before it gets too far. He also said he's now on a journey of discovering how to enter into relationships based on the evidence before him. Sometimes it just takes a little bit of self-awareness to recognize these patterns more clearly.

EVIDENCE-BASED REASONING

When we make decisions using emotional reasoning, we often ignore the evidence and say to ourselves, "Yeah, but I *feel* this way." That's a very nearsighted point of view because it keeps us trapped in the feeling. Decisions made as a direct result of emotional reasoning are often rash decisions that don't come from or serve our Best Self. (Such as when Rocco decided, while using ecstasy, that he was in love with a woman he had just met at a club.)

As you saw in Rocco's example, the "hack" is *evidence-based reasoning*. That's the way to sync back up with your authenticity. In the same way a detective gathers all the evidence before forming an opinion, we must do the same in our decision making. This isn't always easy, given the power of emotions.

Fear keeps us from living a better life. It keeps us from stepping out of our comfort zone, from taking calculated risks, and from experiencing big rewards because, at first, doing those things doesn't *feel* good to us. Fear also causes us to create stories that simply aren't true. Once we are willing to set the fear, or any other emotion keeping us stuck, to the side long enough to examine the evidence, we've already done the hardest part.

For me, as I've built my public persona, I had to face the fact that public speaking didn't feel good. I felt exhausted just thinking about it, and I avoided it for years! I even had a charity that had a traveling self-help event that took place in more than seventy-five cities in conjunction with a pop music tour, and I spoke at only a handful, where I could've spoken at all of them. I didn't feel good speaking; therefore I thought I wasn't supposed to be doing it. I was letting my emotions dictate my reasoning.

When I decided to look at the evidence instead of the emotion, I realized that I had actually been engaging in public speaking for a long time, in the form of presenting new ideas and systems at CAST Centers. And I'd been working with high-profile individuals in group settings for many years. I had actually been honing the skills I would need to appear in more public settings for two decades. Making the jump to the stage and speaking in front of audiences and television viewers was actually far easier than I had imagined. Once I moved past the emotion and relied instead on the evidence, the decision became clear: I was ready to do more public speaking.

Now I am a regular on *Dr. Phil*, and I speak in front of thousands of people at corporate events around the globe, offering my perspective on how they can better their own lives. I also have the podcast *Always Evolving with Coach Mike Bayer*, which allows me to sit down with all kinds of fascinating people and delve into their own decision making. I do live coaching sessions on Instagram and Facebook, as a way to engage more with my audience and give them valuable tools they can apply in their daily lives. And those are just extemporaneous speaking engagements for an audience of a couple hundred up to a few thousand people. You might even have chatted with me in some of those live sessions, or will at some point, and what's fun about those is that they're totally random. Sometimes I'm giving a coaching session, other times we're having a dance-off, and I love that spontaneity.

I also rely on elements of spontaneity when I'm hired to speak at an event. Sometimes we start things off with everyone in the audience snapping a selfie so they can see how they look at themselves at the beginning of the talk versus the end. I sometimes work theatrical elements into my talks as well, mostly because it helps the audience engage and really learn the material and apply it to their life.

The more you do something, the more confident you get, and the more you figure out your own style within it. The more I'm able to be myself, the more people have asked me back, and the more I am able to serve the greater good. All of that is "evidence" that I could use to shift my perspective. You just have to break through the initial story that you tell yourself. Public speaking has become a way of life for me, something I *never* thought would happen!

GUT FEELING? OR EMOTION?

Emotional reasoning can sometimes disguise itself as a gut instinct, so it's important to be able to discern the difference. Research indicates that our brains will create certain types of shortcuts so that we can make decisions quickly. One such shortcut occurs when we quickly or instantly assess probabilities based on how we feel. It is an emotionally fueled reaction to a stimulus. Here's how it plays out.

If you've been bitten by a dog in the past, and a dog is running toward you at the park, then you might experience fear and decide to run in the other direction, even if it's a Chihuahua that wouldn't be able to do much damage anyway. Alternatively, if we've only ever had positive, happy encounters with dogs, we might bend down and greet the bounding dog with open arms. In both instances, we are assigning past emotional experiences (either negative or positive) with people, places, or things to current circumstances. We might assume it's a gut feeling, but we have to pause long enough to ask ourselves if it's really just an emotional reaction and determine whether there's any evidence to support that feeling.

Now, dogs are one thing, but if we are making judgments about ourselves, other people, or specific situations based purely on past emotional experiences, *that's* where we can run into problems and make decisions that are not from our Best Self. Just because we had a rough breakup, and it was a difficult emotional experience, doesn't mean that the new person we've met is also going to break our hearts. This is an example of how we might limit ourselves and miss out on opportunities. The past relationship and the current person we're dating are not the same, and it's not fair to judge one based on an experience with the other.

We have to work to "undo" any inaccurate, emotionally driven shortcuts we might have formed in our brain in an effort to protect ourselves so that we don't unwittingly begin to limit our ability to create a better life.

REGRET-DRIVEN DECISIONS

Regret can be a formidable enemy when it comes to good decision making. Decision theorists have conducted significant research on the role of regret in our choices, and have discovered that it can, indeed, be a powerful motivator. To feel regret means to experience sadness or disappointment over something, especially a missed opportunity. Most of us can easily recall situations in which a poor decision led to painful regret, and so it's quite common to make the decision we believe we will regret the *least*. But that's not always the best decision for us, because it doesn't take into account all of the current, available evidence.

Decision justification theory poses that there are two components to regret as it relates to our decision making. One is comparative; that is, we compare one potential outcome with another and then decide based on which we will regret less. The second is how much we will blame ourselves for a poor choice. It boils down to whether we are going to later judge ourselves harshly for making what we perceive to be a bad decision.

If we make decisions based on regret of past decisions, we are living in the past. And if we make decisions based on fear of future regret, we are not embracing the potential opportunity in front of us. To avoid feeling regret, we can instead choose to make informed, well-thought-out decisions going forward. Our past pain can be a useful tool in creating a better life for ourselves.

ARE YOU RELYING ON EMOTIONAL REASONING? OR EVIDENCE-BASED REASONING?

Now let's take a look at how these two FORCEs might be playing out in your own life. Here is a recap of the two Es and how they differ from each other:

Emotional Reasoning:	Evidence-Based Reasoning:
• Believing our feelings are facts.	• Getting to the truth of the matter.
• Making decisions based on how we feel.	• Making decisions based on the evidence, and not on a feeling.
• Not pushing ourselves to be better, because it doesn't always *feel* good.	• Pushing out of comfort zone in order to cultivate new skills.

EXERCISE

In this chart, you'll see some real-world examples of how the negative FORCE of emotional reasoning can play out, and how we can choose instead to use the positive FORCE of evidence-based reasoning.

EMOTIONAL REASONING	EVIDENCE-BASED REASONING
I don't like presenting my ideas, so I'm just going to stay quiet at work.	When I've had to present something, I've received positive feedback.
I'm angry at my ex, so I'm not even going to try to co-parent.	Children of divorced parents cope better when parents work together to co-parent.
I like how it feels having a good-looking partner, so I won't date people that others don't think are hot.	Looks don't play a big role in long-term happiness in a relationship.

Now it's your turn. Let's put this within the context of your decision making. When it comes to decisions that could lead you toward a better life, what are ways that you've been driven by the negative FORCE of emotional reasoning? Write them in the left column. Then think about the positive FORCE of evidence-based reasoning. When you look at evidence rather than emotion, what's a new way to think about that decision?

EMOTIONAL REASONING	EVIDENCE-BASED REASONING

Let's turn our attention to an area of your life that you want to improve. Remember, this can change and evolve on a regular basis, so if this isn't the same area you were working on yesterday, that's okay! Life is unpredictable, and we need to prioritize certain aspects of life over others based on what is in our own best interest. Your Best Self wants you to be safe, to feel secure and mentally stable, to have meaningful relationships with others, and to live a fulfilling, purpose-driven life. If, for instance, you're experiencing anxiety or stress in the area of your finances, and it's affecting your ability to keep the lights on, then that is likely your most urgent area of focus. Or if your life is severely impacted by your mental health, then that's probably your top priority.

What area of your life is causing you anxiety or stress or just feels off?

_____

_____

_____

_____

_____

What are the emotions you are feeling within those areas? Write
your answers below.

_____

_____

_____

_____

_____

What evidence do you have that supports your feelings in those
areas?

_____

_____

_____

_____

_____

What evidence do you have that does **NOT** support those feelings?

_____

_____

_____

_____

_____

_____

Looking at the overall evidence, what is a decision you could make that is not driven by emotion?

_____

_____

_____

_____

_____

How do you feel now that you're thinking about the situation differently?

_____

_____

_____

_____

_____

We've reached the end of the chapters on the FORCE, and as we move ahead, may the opportunity-minded FORCE be with you now and always! You can return to any of these chapters anytime life deals you an unexpected hand, and you can choose to lean on the FORCE to help you make the decision from your Best Self.

COMING UP . . .
PICKING YOUR TEAM

In the next chapter, you're going to take on the role of team captain in our own life. In making your One Decision toward a better life, you need to have a team on which you can fully rely to give you the advice and opinions that will help you in your decision making. To that end, we're going to take a close look at who is on your decision team, and what roles might be lacking. Let's build a strong team together!

PART 3

CREATING YOUR BETTER LIFE

10

YOUR DECISION MAKING TEAM

Anyone you ask who has been very successful in a certain area of life will say it's the people around them that make it possible. Whether we're talking about a business owner, a religious leader, a government official, a parent, or someone from any other walk of life, they will tell you they got to where they are because of the team around them. No one does it alone, and anyone who thinks they do is giving themselves too much credit. For example, I'm not writing this book in a vacuum; there is an army of people around any author, from the beginning of the process through to the end. You are even part of that army too, as someone who is reading it and using the information in your own life.

Even if a teammate isn't actively helping you make a specific decision, he or she can still be integral to your ability to make your decisions from an authentic place. They might be there to support you emotionally through something, or to help you align with your spirituality, and in so doing, they enable you to be more emotionally and mentally fit to make decisions. Your team can be incredibly helpful, but especially so if you know what you want. And if you're unhappy with an area in your life, but you're not yet sure of what you want in order to improve it, a team can help you make that shift from an obstacle mentality to an opportunity one. If you're trapped in a cycle of negative FORCEs, a team can help pull you back on track.

It's been many years since I've made a decision about something in my life without consulting key team members. I know my skill set, and I know my limitations, so I'm always creating teams that can bring unique perspectives on any given decision. And I'm excited to share with you the formula for building your own Decision Making team.

In *Best Self*, we also discussed your overall team. You may find that many of the folks you picked for your team in that context might apply here too, but there is a fundamental difference. Right now, we need to think about building a team that is ideal for helping you make authentic decisions—a team that will help you take action—and that will support you, no matter the outcome. And because you will be calling upon different people for different types of decisions, we want to be sure you've spent the time identifying and analyzing your teammates so you know whom to go to (and whom to avoid) in any given circumstance. We can't all be experts at everything. You wouldn't call your car mechanic to double-check your tax returns, and you wouldn't call a career mentor to talk about your parenting decisions. Let's make sure you know whom specifically to approach when you're formulating these key decisions in your life. By making sure we have a team in place for all the decisions you need to make, instead of waiting until it's urgent, you're more able to tap into their wisdom and expertise when you really need it.

One of the most important factors in teammates is that they know who you are authentically, and they can help you make decisions from that place. As you know, making decisions as your Best Self trumps the notion of making the "best decision," and the same logic applies to your teammates—it matters who you are and who they are, more than what type of advice they give, or what their background or expertise is in. There will always be a wide range of differing opinions on the best way to accomplish something. That's why figuring out who is the best for you based on who they are is more important. For instance, I'm not always going to be the right life coach for everyone, and that's actually a good thing! No one is right for everyone. The question is, who can I be myself with?

To give you an idea of the types of individuals you might want on your own Decision Making team, I'm going to share a story with you about a friend of mine. I call on him when I'm having a rough day, when I need a little motivation, or when I'm making a life decision and I need someone to help me stay grounded in my Best Self. His name is Deacon. Recently, when I was just minutes away from a presentation in front of my biggest audience yet— three thousand people—I had done my normal prayer and mantra ritual, but I still felt as though I needed to talk to someone. I feel better on a spiritual level when I reach out to people who I know are proud of me no matter what, and who are encouraging. I knew I needed to talk to Deacon.

When I heard his voice on the other end of the line, I knew I'd made the right call. While I knew I could do the presentation, it was him saying, "You've so got this," that gave me that shot of confidence I needed to settle into my Best Self, and let go of the outcome. Deacon is part of the backbone of my One Decision team. I feel totally safe with him; he strengthens me and helps me remember who I am. It all comes down to alignment; he helps me stay aligned with my spirituality.

Deacon's own life story is so inspiring, and it always reminds me that no matter what we're going through, we *can* get to the other side. We all go through struggles in life; we've all experienced hardships from time to time. I find that hearing how other people survived and even came out stronger can stir our spirit and awaken our minds to our own potential. When we're feeling bogged down by life, we can remember that someone, somewhere has been through worse and became better for it. To that end, I asked Deacon to tell me his story in his own words so that I could share it with you. I hope it will serve to inspire you as much as it does me.

DEACON'S STORY

Deacon came from a disadvantaged family. His parents were part of a religious cult when he was born, and he had three older siblings, who were raised in that cult. Shortly after he was born, his mom left the cult and his father, and they moved away. His mom was battling with drug addiction and depression, she wasn't working, and they were living in a shelter for displaced mothers and children.

They lived like this until Deacon was in elementary school. Then, when he was just ten years old, a friend of his was shot. His mom knew it could've easily been him or any of her kids, so she took it as a sign. She believed they needed to get out of there. So they packed everything up, loaded their pickup truck, and took off. The story she told them was that they were camping. They slept in tents, but Deacon remembers there was always food for them. Though he had no idea at the time, the truth was, they were homeless.

Eventually, his mom found them another place to live, but that's around the time he started getting into a lot of trouble. He was basically taking the same path as his mom and his older siblings—using drugs. He thinks he started doing drugs around the age of twelve. He smoked marijuana for the first time in sixth grade, when a lot of kids in his school were doing it too. Being poor and disadvantaged, one tends to find acceptance with other kids in drugs. He was hanging out with all the wrong crowds.

When Deacon was just fourteen years old, he was sent to juvenile detention. They called his dad and told him that either he could pick Deacon up or his son was going into the foster system. He picked him up. His father was financially stable and had a good home, but by this time Deacon knew that he was gay, and his dad was completely against it. His dad was religious, and he did not accept homosexuality. Living with him was difficult not only for that reason but because Deacon had been taken away from everything he had known and put into this situation with a completely new life, this new environment that he wasn't used to. To cope, he started using drugs more heavily.

By eighteen years old, Deacon was selling drugs like ecstasy and LSD to get by. That's when he remembers he started losing all his friends to the addiction. No one wanted to hang out with him because he was so drugged out all the time. So he just used meth in order to not feel the pain of the loneliness.

It wasn't long before he hit rock bottom. He had been staying in friends' places, bouncing around, and he felt suicidal. He had made a few suicide attempts, had even been admitted twice for trying to overdose. One day, he hiked down to the bottom of a canyon. He didn't really have a plan; he was just wandering aimlessly. He eventually nodded off and fell asleep. But because he was coming down from meth, when he'd hiked down to the bottom of the canyon, his body had just shut down and he slept.

When he woke up, it was pouring rain. He was in the middle of nowhere, drenched, freezing cold, and there was blood all over the place. Lying there, he says he just thought—what is going on? He used to be this person that everyone wanted to hang out with; everyone thought he was so cool because he was such a rebel. But he'd lost it all when he'd gotten addicted, and now he was alone.

Lying there, at the bottom of that canyon, was the moment when he finally said no more drugs. Just the thought of ever getting high again made him cringe. He knew he had to get clean and sober.

He started doing dishwashing at some restaurants, and then he decided to go to college. He applied for whatever programs he could get, financial aid (which he did not receive), but he ended up getting a job at a hospital where he made a decent amount of money for the first time. His goal was to become a paramedic. His mom had died of cancer when he was twenty-three, and it was her end-of-life care that made him want to work in the medical field. He went to a program and became a certified nurse's assistant.

At that point, Deacon was doing well. He'd gotten his shit together, as he says, had this great job, was enrolled in college, and was meeting some amazing people. But he was dating someone who was using drugs. Being involved with this guy caused Deacon to relapse. And very quickly thereafter he lost his job.

He knew that he had two choices. He didn't want to hit rock bottom again. He knew he could stop himself before he got any further, and that's what he did. He'd seen both sides; he'd walked the road of loneliness, the countless days of emptiness, drug addiction. And he'd known what it felt like to get praise from the people who saw him doing so well, and he'd experienced the self-gratitude of being able to get a job and then seeing so much and being around doctors and nurses in the hospital. Thinking that way helped him stop and say, "I need to reset myself. I have felt better being sober and working than I ever did using drugs."

It was an easy choice. He ended the relationship and got sober again.

Now he has a totally different career, but he loves it. He gets to travel all over the world. When he thinks about how he got to this point, he says he's learned from other people. He looked at their good habits, their good decisions, and let the role models around him inspire him to improve himself and do something better. Those are all the key players in Deacon's success. And we're not talking about movie stars or wealthy people here. These are just normal people. He has nurse friends and bartender friends who were all amazing to him, and he's adopted that kindness in his own life. They've inspired him to create who he is today.

Despite the problems he had with his dad when he was growing up, in the past couple of years Deacon says that his dad told him he was extremely proud of him. He thinks his dad came to the realization that he could get over it and be part of his life, or not. And he got over the past, and they were able to speak again and be involved in each other's life. Deacon is grateful for that because his father passed away last year.

He knew that there was nothing positive to be gained by holding on to negative feelings, and that nothing would come of holding on to hatred or resentment toward his dad for not being there for him in the way that he needed him. He'd gained his independence, found his way, and Deacon saw no reason to not speak to his dad. So he now has peace about his relationship with his dad.

Deacon told me, "The world is in an odd place and people go through a lot of struggles in life. There was a long time I didn't try and now it's just about finding peace and comfort and enjoying what you have." He says he's enjoyed having his family in his life, and he's actually become the most successful of all his family members. Starting from literally nothing, he's come a long way. In fact, he just bought a house. Having been homeless as a child, he says buying a house was extremely significant for him. He's not rich, but he definitely shares with his family what he can. And that's been what really makes him feel good. He's found that other people's happiness is his happiness.

Deacon had a moment of clarity, which I believe is what happens when God intervenes and we realize we deserve a better life. I love his story because it's about defying the odds. The fact that he makes six figures today, coming from such terrible childhood circumstances, is so inspiring. I mean, his mom was emotionally crippled and addicted to drugs; his dad didn't accept him for who he was . . . Why *would* you want to live? He really had no shot at life. He was alone in the world; he had been given no real tools for living a good life. His future was bleak. Yet, following that moment of clarity he received when he was literally and figuratively at rock bottom, he chose to rise above.

Deacon has a unique ability to see the good in others, and to emulate it. He has such a calm approach to life, so he's always the friend I talk to when there's crazy in my head. With just a few words, or a certain question, he can quiet my mind. He's an essential member of my team, and someone I often consult with when I'm making a decision, whether it's career, life, the internal battles I fight, or even elements of my life that I put into my book. We all need people like Deacon who can speak to our soul and gently remind us of the profound power of the human spirit.

CREATING YOUR DECISION MAKING TEAM

How often do we really take the time to write down the team members in our life? It's such an important exercise, but one that we rarely make time for. The truth is, the majority of us already have great people in our lives, and there's a ton of opportunity to tap into them more, to put more energy into them so that we can really lean on them and utilize them when we are making decisions. Especially when we're making a decision toward crafting a better life, we need to make sure we have a solid team behind us. If it's time to get a better team situation going, your first step will be to evaluate your current team.

Before you write out your current team, let's talk about some roles that people might play on your Decision Making team. This can help you create a more specific and comprehensive list of your teammates. Some roles may apply, some may not, and some of these roles might help you think of someone whom you'd like to add to your Decision Making team. For instance, you might have someone in your universe who is a really good sounding board for you. They listen attentively, they know you well, and they're willing to call you out when you're selling yourself short or missing an opportunity. You may have someone who is inspiring to you and whom you look up to as a spiritual guide. Or you might have a friend who is a connector; they seem to know everyone, and they love getting people together to create new ideas.

Here is a list of roles that might come into effect on your team:

SOUNDING BOARD: This person is a great listener. You can tell them something going on in your life, and they might ask you about it again in six weeks, recalling all the details you shared. They care about you, and rather than offering opinions, they might ask insightful questions to help you discover beliefs you didn't know you had—or even help you out of a confused mindset. You always leave a conversation with this person feeling lighter and less encumbered by worry.

VISIONARY: This person sees you as even greater than you see yourself, and they help you realize your own potential. They can see the opportunities in front of you, now and well into your future, and they are always happy to help you see all the amazing things you are capable of and that you can do in life.

MOTIVATOR: This person gets you fired up and excited to set clear, actionable goals and then crush them. They're the ones who can help you out when you know that you need to take action, but you just haven't done it. Maybe they're doing big things in their own life, or maybe they know just what to say to get you up and moving.

NURTURER: This person always offers a shoulder to cry on; they're the one to go to when the outcome isn't quite as you'd hoped. When you just need a hug and a cup of tea, this person is there for you. The nurturer in your life might do things like send you flowers when you're feeling down, or bring you a home-cooked meal. They enjoy taking care of you, and you know you're always welcome in their world.

BIG-PICTURE THINKER: This person helps you see the big picture of your life when you're caught up in the minutiae. If you're sad, they might point out how many great things you have to be happy about. If you're focusing on the obstacles, they can help you think outside that box. They also help you see how decisions you make now might affect you, for better or worse, in the future.

HELPER: This person would show up to help you move, or you might call this person if you were in trouble in the middle of the night. Not every decision is easy to carry out; sometimes you need logistical help to overcome an obstacle. This person brings no judgment and asks no questions, and there are no strings attached. They are trustworthy and solid.

WISE COUNSEL: This person has lots of wisdom gained on their own walk through life. Maybe they're a generation older, and they've seen a lot in their days on earth. They have a way of simplifying any problem and sharing their own experiences to help guide your decision. With hindsight, they can see where opportunities arise from the most unexpected places. This person can also help you see through any shortsighted emotional reasoning. They may even help you in your spiritual practice.

CONNECTOR: This person gets a thrill out of connecting people to one another and making "worlds collide." Whenever you bring up a topic of interest, they always seem to know several people with similar interests, some of which may be great, but others may not be. They seem to know everyone, and they have an uncanny ability to know whom you might get along with, or who might be helpful to you. They can even help you build your team further.

FUN MAKER: This person is the one you call when you just want to have fun. They love to laugh, meet new people, and just be happy wherever they are. They can help you cut loose and unwind so that your mind and spirit can relax. They are more likely to have a relaxed mindset, and may be able to help you get there too.

ADVISER: This person loves nothing more than sharing new information with others, so you might come to this person if you need to learn something in order to make a decision—especially when you have some serious fact-finding to do. It's wise to select an adviser who is an expert in the area that encompasses your decision. For instance, if it's a financial decision, someone with a background or successful track record in accounting or investing would make a great adviser. Or if it's a health decision, then a physician or someone in the health-care industry would be a wise choice for an adviser.

STUDENT: This person has a student mentality and they love learning from you. This role is great because it gives you the opportunity to share your wisdom. And their curiosity may help pique your own. One thing to be aware of with this role is some students have  been known for cheating, and in certain cases in business they may replicate or take your ideas. Just be mindful of that risk.

THERAPIST: Not in the literal sense, as in having a PhD in psychology, but this is the person you can approach to get some no-nonsense objective advice. This person can offer clarity, but watch out because they might also offer confusion. The challenge with this role is they don't have any official training. So they might be advising you based on their own story.

You might have other roles in mind that the people in your life play for you; by all means, write them down! This list is just a jumping-off point for you to consider. Another great question to ask yourself is which of these roles you fill for others in your life. And are there any new roles you'd like to start playing?

A WORD ON AGENDAS

The term "agenda" has gotten a bad reputation. It means "the underlying intentions or motives of a particular person or group," but those intentions or motives are not necessarily nefarious. I believe, most of the time, people's agendas are positive. They just might be self-serving. But just because someone has an agenda that is self-serving doesn't mean it can't also be helpful to you. I've found in my own life that when people's agendas align, teams can get so much more

(continued)

done. Agendas can be helpful in collaboration. You run into trouble only when agendas are not aligned.

For instance, if a woman is trying to decide whether her current boyfriend is husband material, and she's asking for people's opinions, she needs to be careful to consider their agendas. Perhaps her mom just desperately wants a grandbaby, and figures this guy is "as good as any" to help her achieve that agenda. Well, her agenda and her daughter's agenda are not aligned in that case. But perhaps her friend whom she's known since first grade just wants what is best for her; then their agendas are aligned and her advice is more meaningful.

When we feel vulnerable, as we often do when we are making a decision, we don't want to have to deal with other people's agendas in our decision making. So, as you build your One Decision team, be mindful of agendas. Ask yourself, "What might this person's agenda be, and does it align in some way with my own?" before you approach them for counsel on any decisions you need to make in your life.

BUILDING YOUR DECISION MAKING TEAM

Now that you have thought about the specific roles that you want on your team, let's get down onto paper everyone who is within your decision-making universe. Some of these teammates will come to mind very easily. For instance, if you tend to always talk to one or two people, perhaps a spouse or a sibling, about many of your decisions, then he or she will certainly go on your list. But I also want you to think about other, less obvious decision-making teammates you might have. Perhaps you listen to podcasts of a specific genre, and often base decisions in those areas on the information or advice you've heard in the podcast. Maybe you follow certain influencers on social media who fire you up or point you in a new direction on a regular basis. If that's the case, make sure you include those folks in your list too. Again, this is about identifying the Decision Making team that is authentic to *you* and that will help you stay within your Best Self as you make decisions in your life.

Keep in mind that these are the people who will be there for you not only as you are actively making decisions but also as you experience the outcomes. Some of the members of your team may help you stay accountable to your intentions when you have moments of questioning. For example, maybe it's a nurturer who talks you through the moments when you consider getting back into a relationship you left because it wasn't in your best interest, but you're having a moment of loneliness. Or it could be the big-picture thinker who reminds you why you changed career tracks to do something that is more meaningful to you, even though it's hard to start at something new. Perhaps it's a motivator who joins you for walks or an exercise class when you feel like you aren't losing weight despite making healthier choices. Whatever those roles are for you, make sure you include them below.

Fill in your team here:

MY OVERALL DECISION MAKING TEAM

_____

_____

_____

_____

_____

_____

_____

_____

_____

Thinking about the area of life you're looking to improve right now, let's build your team. If, for example, you're focusing your current attentions on finding a healthy relationship, you can look at your universe and see who would be most helpful when it comes to making decisions on dating—maybe it's a motivator or a big-picture thinker. Or if you're looking to change jobs, perhaps you need a connector on your decision team, and someone with some sage wisdom because they've likely been in the same spot you are right now. If you've got some urgent financial challenges you need to overcome, you might need a motivator or a helper. The most important aspect of all these teammates, however, is that they know who you truly are, and that they are able to help you stay rooted in that authenticity. I can't say it enough; *that's* what matters most about your team.

Another important aspect of building your team is knowing whom *not* to include. You can love someone very much and have an awesome relationship with them, and they can even be someone who knows you very well, but they are just not equipped to help you when it comes to your business, for instance. While they might think they know a lot about business, their advice may not be exactly right for your situation. They mean well, but they aren't helpful. You need to be able to identify who those people are. In my own life, if I'm feeling confused about a situation, I sometimes go to too many people instead of sitting, meditating, getting clarity, or speaking to just one or two people.

If, for instance, you are deciding whether to go back to school, the team you assemble might be made up of your accountant, who can help you sort out how to afford the cost of school, or other people in the field you want to study, but you might not include your parents on that particular team. They may not be able to offer helpful advice. The point is, don't seek advice from people who aren't equipped to advise you in that area.

Also keep in mind that the people on your decision team may not be "regulars" in your life. I may only see some of the people on my team once in a while, whereas others I might see and talk to all the time. The same is true for you. Some of these people might be long-distance, or as we discussed earlier, they might be hosts of shows that you've never met before! But they can still be on your team, in that you might lean on their content or wisdom to help you.

With any given decision you need to make to better your life, the first place to look is within yourself. The majority of decisions in life actually don't require other people, but when we're feeling indecisive, it's wonderful to already have a team from which to choose people who can help us get the clarity we need. But we all do need support; sometimes we need support to be ourselves, and sometimes we need support toward taking specific action. You might be reading this right now and thinking that you don't have enough people in your life who truly know who you are. We are all on this infinite journey of self-discovery, and we all need people who love us for who we are. Community builds us up and helps us navigate our way through our lives. People go to recovery meetings, church, or self-help workshops and conferences for *community*.

Everyone needs a team.

COACH MIKE ON YOUR TEAM

I also want you to know that you should count *me* in on your decision team. The content I create, the interviews I conduct on my podcast—it's all information that you can use to better your life. I love hearing inspiring stories and feeling motivated by choices other people have made in their lives, and I'm guessing you do too. I make a daily decision to put positive content into the world. As you make decisions in your own life, and as you become more aware of your ability to create change in your life, I hope you'll lean on me and the information and ideas I'm sharing to move forward in new directions. You can find me on any of the social media platforms @CoachMikeBayer.

HAVING A SOLID TEAM MEANS BEING A SOLID TEAMMATE

It's important to remember that you're not the only one with a team; we all have teams, so you're very likely on other people's teams as well. And we don't have to try to be all things to all people; in other words, we each have our own individual roles to play. So, when you think about showing up as a great teammate for others, ask yourself which specific role is actually suited to you. The goal is to love them for who they truly are, and help them stay on that path.

When you feel good about what you're bringing to a teammate, they will feel that positivity. Everyone wins. It feels so good when others see us for who we are, and so let's take this as a good reminder to help others in our lives feel seen for who they truly are.

11

TAKING AUTHENTIC ACTION

By this point, you understand the FORCE and how it works in your life, and with that understanding I hope you've begun to hone the ability to see when you're being driven by a negative FORCE, to hack it into its flip-side positive FORCE. You understand how it's your perception that can change an obstacle into opportunity, and, importantly, you understand that you don't need to go through this journey alone. We are stronger when we have a team helping us keep aligned. I hope that as you've read these pages and completed the exercises, you have felt empowered to see the world, and see your life, as your authentic self, your Best Self. All these ideas and exercises are meant to help you take action as that Best Self—not just to focus inward on yourself, but to get your whole life into alignment with it.

As you've been reading this book, I'll bet you've had some moments where you think, "Yes! I've totally felt that way!" or "Yep,

I've been stuck in that mode of thinking before!" We've all experienced the results of the negative FORCEs in our lives before. It's okay! We're human! What's important is to realize that we've also witnessed ourselves rising up and taking hold of opportunities rather than relinquishing control to a negative FORCE. In other words, you've done this before; you have taken something that you could've perceived as an obstacle, risen above it, and grabbed hold of an opportunity instead.

I'll give you a few examples from my own life:

OBSTACLE: Becoming addicted to meth, and believing my addiction would always control me.

OPPORTUNITY: Realizing that others had gotten sober before, so I could too.

ONE DECISION: Call my parents; check into treatment.

OUTCOME: I got sober, and I have eighteen years of sobriety.

BONUS: I became a counselor, and later founded the dual diagnosis treatment center CAST Centers.

OBSTACLE: I had disk replacement surgery in my neck.

OPPORTUNITY: I was asked to appear on *Dr. Phil* three days after the surgery.

ONE DECISION: I decided to go for it. Sure, I could have chosen to just sit in my house, mindlessly bingeing Netflix. Or I could choose to throw on a turtleneck to cover the bandages and push myself to inspire and help others alongside Dr. Phil. Either way, I would have been sitting, whether on a stage or at home. My physician said it was fine as long as I wasn't moving too much, so I went ahead and I was able to use this as an opportunity to go on television and feel proud of myself.

OUTCOME: It was a great episode, and hopefully the last time I ever wear a turtleneck on TV!

BONUS: Realizing that I'm more physically resilient than I ever knew!

OBSTACLE: I was offered a book deal, which is amazing, but I'd never done well in school, I'm dyslexic, and I have ADD, so I couldn't imagine actually writing all of my ideas and concepts in the form of a book. In fact, it was my worst nightmare.

OPPORTUNITY: See above! The very thing I was first viewing as an obstacle was, in fact, a giant opportunity. Others believed in me wholeheartedly, and ultimately I realized I had something to say.

ONE DECISION: I did it; I wrote *Best Self*, even though it took longer for me to write than it might take other authors, but who cares!

OUTCOME: I became a *New York Times* bestselling author. And then I wrote a workbook companion, and the book you're reading right now! Bam! Three books in less than two years.

OBSTACLE: I come from divorced parents, have siblings who had compulsive, self-destructive behaviors, and grew up in an emotionally challenging environment.

OPPORTUNITY: Learning how to work through those challenges from my youth could give me a better life not defined by struggle.

ONE DECISION: Go to therapy; work through my past experiences to become better for myself and to help others.

OUTCOME: Healing, personal growth, compassion for others.

BONUS: I'm a better and more understanding person now because of the challenges I faced.

Now, I want you to write out at least three examples from your own life of experiences or situations that you could have perceived as obstacles but that you have turned into opportunities. Then, as I did in my examples, write out the One Decision you made, the outcome, and any bonus to that outcome that you might have experienced.

OBSTACLE:	
OPPORTUNITY:	
ONE DECISION:	
OUTCOME:	
BONUS:	

OBSTACLE:	
OPPORTUNITY:	
ONE DECISION:	
OUTCOME:	
BONUS:	

OBSTACLE:	
OPPORTUNITY:	
ONE DECISION:	
OUTCOME:	
BONUS:	

As you can see, you have already overcome many of your own obstacles or circumstances, so you know firsthand that you are capable. And is there any way you could have predicted the outcomes you listed? No way, right? That's where I'd like you to focus your attention throughout this chapter. Outcomes are out of our control, and we never know what to expect. In fact, much of the time, when we look back on an outcome, we are able to identify a "bonus" that is far and away more amazing than we could have imagined or predicted. Who knew that having a learning disability and ADD would make me more relatable to other people who struggled growing up? And I couldn't have known that as a result of playing basketball as a child, I developed a natural tendency to stay healthy and active throughout my life; that's an unforeseen bonus. Use the potential for bonus outcomes as inspiration for continuing your commitment to viewing life as an opportunity, and making your One Decision as your Best Self.

The universe is not trying
to defeat you.

On the contrary! The universe wants you to win, as you've just proven to yourself. Remember: it's not about the universe giving you what you want right now, because there are times when the thing we really want might not actually be in our best interest. We may think we really want a particular job for a variety of reasons, but there's actually a better one that will become available in a few weeks that we couldn't possibly know about. We may not be able to see the reasons why we didn't get that job, but we have to trust that the universe knows what's best. And by just being ourselves instead of trying to force an outcome, we take our focus off what we think we want in the moment and relinquish control, thus opening ourselves up to unimaginable possibilities. The point is, when we are taking authentic action, even if the outcome isn't exactly what we'd pictured, there will likely be something even more awesome in store for us. That's the universe at work.

DECISIONS FOR YOUR
BETTER LIFE

Whether you're sick and tired of being sick and tired, you feel like you need to do something to protect yourself, to enhance your life, or to create more love and peace in your life—it always begins with your One Decision to act as your Best Self. When we get out of alignment, it's often because we aren't following our truth, heart, or destiny. But now that you are making decisions as your Best Self, you can rest assured that your next steps will be in alignment with your own authenticity.

Now you need to ask yourself, what do you truly want to make a decision, or decisions, around? Since you started the work in this book, your thoughts on this might have shifted. It could be because of a shift in your perception, or it could be that life evolved and now there's a new set of decisions to make in your life.

I want you to create a list of decisions that you can make in your life that you know are in your best interest. They may mean a certain relationship needs to end, or they may mean a new journey is beginning. But if you make five authentic decisions that would better your life right now, you will begin to experience significant changes.

As we've discussed, we make decisions all day long, but how often do we really sit down and carefully consider our decisions? We're so often managing our own lives instead of slowing down and making decisions that would lead to a better life. This is an opportunity to get out of making reactionary decisions, instead of making decisions out of our power and authenticity. And that's why I believe you're going to be in a different spot if you start right now with making purposeful decisions.

Write down up to five decisions you can make right now to create positive change in your life.

MY DECISIONS

1. _____

   _____

2. _____

   _____

3. _____

   _____

4. _____

   _____

5. _____

   _____

Throughout this book, we've been focusing on how to get you to think differently. You've familiarized yourself with the FORCEs in your head, and you're thinking opportunity over obstacle. Now it's time to *act* differently.

Whatever was holding you back before is no longer in your way. You now have the tools to clear out the wreckage of your past, to see the opportunity in everything, so what are you waiting on? This is your time to step out in faith and see what happens. Say out loud, "It's my time!" Say it again. **"It's *my* time!"** Let's say you make that phone call but you get rejected. Remember, rejection is God's protection, and it means a new opportunity is right around the corner. But you'll never know if you don't take that first step. Do you want to buy a house, but you've been too afraid to take the risk? Start looking at homes *today*. No one says you have to pull the trigger, but you can at least start the process. What I'm saying is—don't delay.

Take the first step.

In this chapter, I'm going to give you methods for putting your decisions into immediate action. And underneath it all is an important reality: life is so impermanent, and what we're striving for today might very well shift. Maybe we'll see an opportunity tomorrow that we couldn't have envisioned today; thus we'll need to pivot our actions accordingly. This is the reason why I don't really love traditional "goal setting"; it can be very rigid in that we get singularly focused on one specific goal, and we run the risk of missing out on potentially bigger and better goals. That's why I want you to have these tools for making decisions to better your life, but always with your eyes and heart open to new decisions you might want to make along the way.

You've decided to have a better life, so let's *do* this.

IDENTIFY WHAT ISN'T WORKING

Now that you understand *why* you're making the decisions you're making, it's time to step into action mode. As a life coach, I focus on behavior because in order to create change in our life, we have to first make a decision and then *behave* our way to success. But sometimes, especially if we've been doing the same things for a long time, it's tough to know exactly what we need to do differently in order to bring our One Decision to life. So I like to start by identifying behavior that is *not* working for us.

A straightforward example to consider is this: let's say you are unhappy with your weight and you want to trim down. We would investigate your current behavior that could be keeping you overweight. I like to write this as a cycle, because one behavior tends to lead to another, to another, and they keep us stuck in the same circle, just going around and around. Here's one way to envision it:

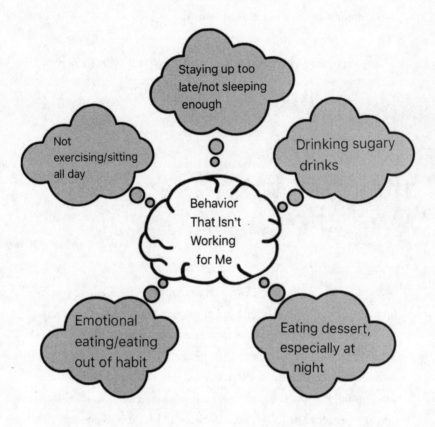

When you break it down, this is just a matter of looking at your daily routines and identifying behavior that is keeping you from changing—in this case, that's keeping you from losing weight. Knowing what *isn't* working is the first step toward identifying what behaviors you need to stop doing.

Now, I want you to look at the list of your own decisions in the last exercise and think about what is not working in terms of how you are approaching that part of your life. I am sure some of the items on the list are not new decisions you are going to make, so let's identify what you have done in the past that hasn't worked for you. Write a list of your behaviors that are keeping you "stuck" in the area of life you want to change, or that are keeping you from being able to create the change you want. What are some things you're doing that are perpetuating the problem area in your life?

Now that you can see the behaviors that are not working, you know which behaviors you need to *stop* doing in order to act on your decisions and improve your life. Writing it all out instead of just thinking about it is so helpful. When we are confronted with our behaviors that aren't working in our life, it's much easier to see where we need to change our daily decisions in order to support our new goal.

IDENTIFYING NEW BEHAVIORS TO ADOPT

Anytime we *stop* doing specific behaviors that have been preventing us from positive change, it is so helpful to replace them with behaviors that *will* help us move forward. We never really "break" a habit; we simply replace it with a new one. So this is our chance to stop bad habits or choices and replace them with ones that are in our best interest.

You see, your One Decision is surrounded by many uniting decisions. They represent the actions you need to take or the behaviors you need to adopt in order to get you where you want to go in your life.

For instance, if we want to improve our social life and create more meaningful friendships, maybe instead of meeting people out at bars, we can meet people through our similar interests, like in a running club or an art class. The behavior we need to "start" could be to plug into community activities like those.

In the weight loss example, perhaps we need to begin to pre-pare meals in advance so that we aren't deciding what to eat when we're starving and just want a greasy cheeseburger. And maybe since we stopped eating snacks out of habit, we are sure to always have a bottle of purified water on hand so that we can sip on that instead. Another behavior that would help in the weight loss goal is to choose a realistic workout routine.

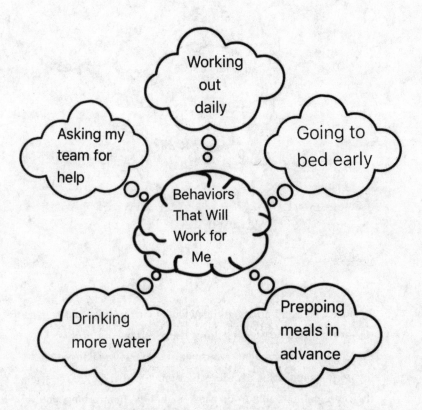

Now it's your turn. What behaviors do you need to start implementing in your life in order to support your One Decision?

Once we begin implementing behaviors in our lives that help us rather than hinder us, something really interesting occurs. They take on a natural momentum. As you see yourself making and acting on the supporting decisions that move you closer to the goal, the more you are able to do those activities. Before long, you've started to program your daily behavior in a way that supports your One Decision without your even having to try very hard. It all begins by writing it down and getting started.

FIRING UP YOUR ONE DECISION TEAM

Once you have a clear idea of the behaviors you need to stop doing and the ones you need to start doing, the next step is to get your One Decision team involved. If you flip back to chapter 10, you'll see there are many roles people might play on your team, and depending on what you're looking to accomplish, you may need just one of those roles, or you may need to fill several of them, especially when you're first starting out.

For instance, in the weight loss example, you might need a couple of different "wise counsel" teammates who can advise you on the specific decisions you need to make around your eating and exercise plans. These might be experts to work with one-on-one, or it might be someone you follow on Instagram who always has great diet or exercise advice. It could even be that friend who lost fifty pounds and they can advise you on how they did it. And you might need a "helper" in the form of someone to whom you can be accountable for all the uniting decisions you're making around your new lifestyle. You might text or email this person daily with an update on your progress, or they might check in with you once a week to see how you're doing.

Choose your specific team for this goal carefully, and then rely on them to help you stay on track.

BRINGING IT ALL TOGETHER

Now it's time to envision your One Decision action plan so that you see how it all comes together. In the sample flowchart below, you'll see "Lose Weight" in the first box. That's your One Decision. Then you'll see "Create Decision Team" and "Stop This, Start That." Those are the two overarching steps we've discussed so far. Then, to the far right, you'll see a list of your teammates on the top, and the specific behaviors you're going to start or stop.

This flowchart will look different for everyone, and for every One Decision we make in our lives. Creating change in our lives requires us to be intentional about our decisions, and I find the best way to follow through on our intentions is to write it out so that we can refer to it for reminders and motivation along the way.

Here's the sample:

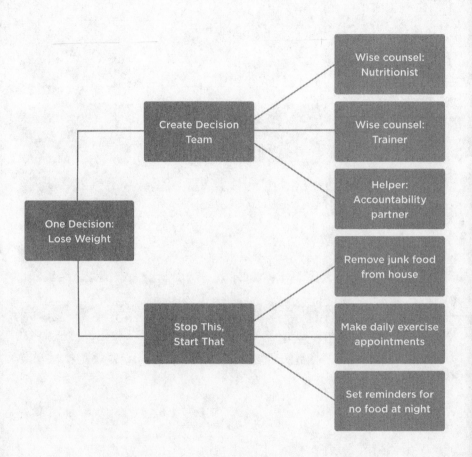

Now it's your turn. You may want to do this on a separate piece of paper or in your journal. But here's a blank flowchart in case it's easier to fill in here:

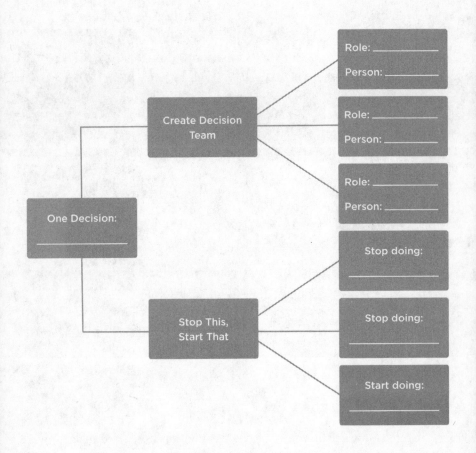

LET THE UNIVERSE DECIDE

Making your One Decision, and all of the uniting decisions around it, can be exhilarating. You've acknowledged that you hold the power to change your life for the better, and you are taking action toward it right now. That should feel amazing. But I want to bring to your attention the imperative, final step in this process.

> Let the universe decide
> the outcome.

When I was at Fordham University, before I got sober, there was a paper I was supposed to write in our philosophy class. The idea was to write about one topic from the perspective of two famous philosophers debating but in a modern-day setting. Essentially the question was this: If these philosophers were alive today, how would they argue their positions?

The whole year had been leading up to this paper, and to be honest, I had ditched half of the classes and I'd shown up stoned to the other half. I guess you could say I had a stoner's philosophical thinking, which means I'd get high and then all of a sudden think I'd connected the dots on solving world peace or that I'd discovered the meaning of life. So, not exactly the types of answers my professor was looking for.

Long story short, I had this paper due in twenty-four hours, and no joke it would have taken me several weeks to write it. My older brother, David, was friends with these twins named Daniel and Jeremy Lehrer, whose names I mention with permission. They were total geniuses and still are. I called them up and begged them to write the paper for me because, otherwise, I was screwed. My fear was that if I didn't turn in a great paper, then I would fail and have to take the class all over again. So they did me the favor and wrote the paper. When I read it over, I was amazed at the creative idea they'd come up with. They pitted the two philosophers against each other—I think it was Descartes and Socrates— and they were just going at it, giving all this great evidence that proved their point and perspective. I didn't change one single thing about the paper; I just turned it in.

When the professor handed it back a week later, there was a big red F at the top of the first page. Of course, the professor knew I had not written one word of that paper. And the worst part was— that grade made up one-third of our overall grade in the class. My transcript certainly suffered for that one.

Fast-forward several years to a psychopharmacology course I was taking as part of a program to become a drug and alcohol counselor. This was after I'd gotten sober, so my decision making was no longer clouded by substances. Nevertheless, I made an impulsive decision. It wasn't premeditated in the least, and even as I was doing it, I knew I was acting impulsively. But we were taking a test, and my eyes flickered over to the answer that the woman next to me was writing.

You know what's coming next.

Though I had studied hard for this test, and I knew most of the answers, I still just impulsively copied her answers. At the end of the exam, I turned it in to the professor, but as I was walking out the door, I made another impulsive decision. I turned on my heel and went straight up to the professor. "I copied someone's answers on this exam. I cheated," I blurted out. I had no idea what was coming next, and I didn't really care; all I knew was that I felt instantly relieved. The professor was visibly taken aback, her eyes wide and her brow furrowed confusedly. I don't know if she thought I was kidding, or I was crazy, or what.

"On *this* exam, that you just turned in?" she asked.

"Yes. I saw someone's answer and I just wrote it down. I'm sorry," I said.

She nodded and just said, "Thank you, Mike." And I left the room.

The following week in class, we got our exam grades. I was stunned. I'd received an A. After class, I went up to the professor, and before I could say anything, she said, "Thank you for your honesty," and then she turned to consult with another student.

As you can see, I was impulsive in my decision making. Cheating, clearly, is never okay. And I knew that. But rather than let it go and just wish I hadn't done it, or let it hang over me like a black cloud, I immediately owned it. Now, the professor could have spoken to the dean, and who knows what could have happened then? But the truth was, whatever the consequence had been, it would have been okay with me, because I had told the truth about my poor decision. The universe decided I was going to be spared, and I was grateful for that.

I know that people *can* change. And when we change, our decisions change and the world around us changes too. Now that you have discovered how to make decisions as your Best Self, you too have the power to change any part of your life you choose.

We can control a lot, specifically our behavior, but we simply cannot control or predict outcomes. Period. But rather than sitting around in fear, wondering how things are going to turn out, we can choose to relax into it. We can be in a peaceful state of mind, and because we've made decisions as our Best Self, we can let the universe decide the result. Now, I know it can feel a little strange, after all this work we've done on ourselves and all this planning, to then just "let go and let God." But there's such freedom in it because the truth is, the universe might just have something planned for us that is infinitely more awesome than what we expected. We know that something will change, because *we've* changed, and it could be far and away better than what we anticipated.

You've made your One Decision, which is to approach all decisions as your Best Self, and you're doing what it takes to bring it to life. That's what you came here to do. The rest is in the hands of the universe, or God, or however you think of the higher power. Your job is to feel confident and self-assured that you carefully made your decision from your Best Self, and viewed through the lens of opportunity.

Right now, as a symbol of your willingness to let the universe decide, I encourage you to say a mantra out loud. For me, I like saying mantras in the mirror because I can connect with my own eyes, and it feels like I'm speaking to my spirit. I'll give you a sample mantra below, but feel free to write this in your own words so that it resonates within you:

With an opportunity mindset,
I have made my decision as my Best Self.
I know what I have to do.
I now choose to let the universe decide the outcome.
I surrender control, and I choose to have peace.

Write it down and keep it close so that you can return to it anytime you feel yourself needing a gentle reminder. The longest journey that we're all on is from the head to the heart. One way to make it easier is to keep your heart open so you're fully who you are meant to be. It's also important to remember that you have a lot to be grateful for today, and that you deserve to make decisions that are from your heart in this limited time that you have on this earth. And when I say heart, I'm referring to your love for life, the excitement for opportunity, the ability to overcome challenges, the freedom to get to the other side of anything, and the resilience you feel when you're there.

UNAPOLOGETICALLY AUTHENTIC

If you've gotten this far in the book, you're incredible. I know that a lot of people don't get through this type of book, one that challenges you to really look at yourself and dig deep. It can be daunting, but you did it. I truly hope if you've learned nothing else, that you've learned this: who you *are* is exactly who you *should be*. If that's the case, then I've done my job.

Now you can move forward in your life unapologetically living as your Best Self.

As we talked about in the very beginning of this book, living authentically is a decision we make every single day. And we will not always succeed at it. I shared with you some of the ways I've gotten off course in my own life, and it will inevitably happen again. But now you have the tools to find your way back, to tap into the positive FORCEs, and to make decisions as your Best Self again. I'm here to help too. Please feel free to follow me on social media, on all channels. My team and I have created a *One Decision* book club, where you'll discover a diverse community of people. It's a fun place, and an empowering place. I hope you'll join. Just look for @CoachMikeBayer.

Until next time, I'll leave you with these words.

MAKE A DECISION . . .

TO NEVER GIVE UP ON YOURSELF

TO EMBRACE YOUR UNIQUENESS

TO SILENCE YOUR EXCUSES

TO JUDGE THE TASTE OF FOOD BUT NOT
PEOPLE

TO BE IN THE SOLUTION

TO SEE YOUR PAST STRUGGLE AS A SIGN OF
YOUR OWN RESILIENCE

TO SPEND TIME DOING WHAT LIFTS YOU UP

TO LIFT OTHER PEOPLE UP

TO LOVE UNCONDITIONALLY

TO TELL YOUR STORY

TO LOVE YOURSELF

ACKNOWLEDGMENTS

First, I'd like to thank Brian Tart, Emily Wunderlich, and the rest of my stellar team at Viking. You've been such strong partners in the creation of this book. I want to express my gratitude to Jan Miller for being a ball of motivation and unparalleled tenaciousness. My agent, Lacy Lalene Lynch, has played a key role in my writing of this book. Lacy, you have encouraged me to write from a place of honesty, and to share my truth. With zero judgment along the way, a seemingly bottomless well of patience, willingness to listen, and keen ability to help me arrive at decisions as well as write about them, you have championed this content from day one. And Dabney Rice, I see your meaningful contributions behind the scenes, and I appreciate your dedication.

None of this would be possible without Dr. Phil, who has pushed me, taught me, and made me an overall better navigator in life. I feel lucky to call you a friend. Robin McGraw, I am continuously amazed by your insightful and intuitive nature. Thank you for being so inspirational to me and to everyone who knows you. And to everyone in the Dr. Phil "universe," every single one of you has been incredibly generous and kind. Carla Pennington, you and your team of top-notch producers have set the bar so high that it has made me raise my own game and pushed me to get better and better.

My brother, David, is forever reminding me that my greatest gift is who I am. My dad, Ronald, you're an incredible sounding board and wise counsel. And to my mom, Aina, you've instilled a persistent curiosity in me. I'm grateful.

I also would like to acknowledge the amazingly talented Hurtado brothers: Nikko, for using his story to inspire others, and his brother Mathew, for collaborating and creating all of the illustrations for *One Decision*.

Seti, you always help me keep it simple and remind me of my art. Mike Piacentino, you help me process things and you're always consistent—thank you. And to everyone whose stories appear in the pages of this book, I appreciate you taking the time and graciously allowing me to tell your real, true stories. Your contributions are priceless to me. I want to mention my internal Coach Mike team of Samson Motavassel, Tony Zuniga, and Misty Foster. You guys have evolved with me and made me better for it. To my mental health leadership team at CAST Centers, headed up by Robert Lien, Mike Rizzo, and Mardet Homans—you've shown up in so many awesome ways while I've been working on this book, and I appreciate it more than you know.

For relentlessly helping me bring my concepts to life and articulate them in real and practical ways, and for being my guinea pig by applying so many of the ideas in this book to her own life, thank you, Lisa Clark.

Finally, saving the best for last, thank you to everyone who has reached out to me and shared how some aspect of content I've put out into the universe has helped you in your lives. *You* are the reason I do any of this. I am so fueled and inspired by your willingness to listen, to learn, to adapt, and to evolve. I'm honored you've committed to go on another journey of self-discovery via *One Decision*, and I truly hope you create the "better life" you so richly deserve.

NOTES

CHAPTER 6: OVERGENERALIZING OR OBJECTIVE THINKING

127 **"drawing a conclusion or making a statement":** Oxford English Dictionary, "Overgeneralize," https://www.lexico.com/en/definition/overgeneralize.

144 **Based on which examples:** Johan E. Korteling, Anne-Marie Brouwer, and Alexander Toet, "A Neural Network Framework for Cognitive Bias," Frontiers in Psychology 9 (2018).

CHAPTER 7: RIGID MINDSET OR RELAXED MINDSET

161 **In fact, there was a study:** Jeremy A. Frimer, Linda J. Skitka, and Matt Motyl, "Liberals and Conservatives Are Similarly Motivated to Avoid Exposure to One Another's Opinions," *Journal of Experimental Social Psychology* 72 (2017): 1–12, www.sciencedirect.com/science/article/abs/pii/S0022103116304024.

CHAPTER 9: EMOTIONAL REASONING OR EVIDENCE-BASED REASONING

211 **Al-Anon Family Groups:** Al-Anon Family Groups, Media Kit, al-anon.org/media -kit/.

212 **According to the National Survey:** Rachel N. Lipari, PhD, and Struther L. Van Horn, MA, "Children Living with Parents Who Have a Substance Use Disorder," The CBHSQ Report, Aug. 24, 2017, www.samhsa.gov/data/sites/default/files /report_3223/ShortReport-3223.html.

223 **It is an emotionally fueled reaction:** Eric Wargo, "The Mechanics of Choice," As-

sociation for Psychological Science, Dec. 28, 2011, www.psychologicalscience.org /observer/the-mechanics-of-choice.

CHAPTER 10: YOUR DECISION MAKING TEAM

249 **"the underlying intentions or motives":** Oxford English Dictionary, 'Agenda," https://www.lexico.com/en/definition/agenda.